Basic Blues
For Guitar

By **Fred Sokolow**

Electric Blues • Blues Rock • Country Blues • Bottleneck Blues • Jazz Blues

Edited by Ronny S. Schiff
Cover Design by Elyse Morris Wyman
Photography and Production by E.K. Waller

ISBN 978-0-7935-4320-5

Schiff / Sokolow Publishing

EXCLUSIVELY DISTRIBUTED BY

HAL•LEONARD®

7777 W. BLUEMOUND RD. P.O. BOX 13819 MILWAUKEE, WI 53213

Visit Hal Leonard Online at: **www.halleonard.com**

CONTENTS

This is a complete blues guitar book. It starts with "basics" for those who never before picked up a guitar. If you know how to play, there's still a treasure trove of information covering all the styles and forms of "blues-playing." The book virtually presents a history of blues guitar . . . from its content you can learn the techniques of:

Early Bottleneck (slide guitar)—bluesmen such as Robert Johnson and Bukka White—the roots of blues guitar.

Black Rural Guitar Pickers—such as Big Bill Broonzy, Lightnin' Hopkins and other finger-picking, folk-blues guitarists.

Modern Electric Guitarists—such as B.B. King, Buddy Guy—electric slide guitarists such as Muddy Waters and Elmore James.

Early Rock Guitar—the styles of Chuck Berry and other guitarists of the 50's.

Contemporary Rock, Soul and Acid-Rock players who use blues guitar styles in a pop music frame-work—Eric Clapton, Jimi Hendrix, Duane Allman, etc.—including country-rock and softer styles, and modern slide guitar.

Jazz Guitar—applying blues styles to jazz and swing progressions.

Three dozen exercises exemplifying the above styles are recorded for you on the tape, and they are written out in regular music notation as well as tablature. Chord grids are added to facilitate your learning process. You'll find the lead guitar on one track and the accompaniment on the other. Both parts are written out. All this will make your practice session easier!

"Blues guitar" is universal! You can use it to play rock, soul, jazz, country—any American music style. Herein, you'll find the scales, fingerboard charts, chords, "licks," theory—all the vocabulary, sentence-structure and rules of grammar you need for any area of your guitar picking interest.

Once you've learned some basic scales, you'll be amazed at the number of different ways you can use them—in all styles and all keys and all over the fretboard. But let's start at the beginning.

At the beginning, you tune up the guitar . . .

HOW TO READ TABLATURE

Each exercise in this book is written both in tablature *and* in the standard music notation. You can use either system.

In tablature, the 6 lines on the staff represent the 6 strings of the guitar as follows:

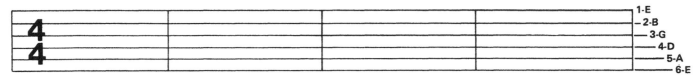

A number on a line tells you where to fret the string.

This example:

means "play the 4th string on the 2nd fret."

This example:

means "play the 2nd string unfretted."

Notice that the staff above is divided into 4 measures. The time signature at the far left tells you two things about the timing: the top number says there are 4 beats in each measure; the bottom number says that a quarter note gets one beat. The tunes in this book are mostly in 4/4 or 6/8 time. Here is a measure in 4/4 with 4 quarter notes:

Eighth notes (with a flag on their stems) are played with half the time value of quarter notes—it takes 8 eighth notes to fill a measure in 4/4 time. Two or more eighth notes are connected this way: 5   6

Here's a single eighth note: 4

Here's a measure in 6/8 time. It totals 6 beats in all, with each eighth note counting for one beat (the quarter note counts for two beats)

"Sixteenth" notes get half the value of quarter notes, and look like this: 3   or this: 4   6

"Rests" on the staff indicate pauses of different time value.

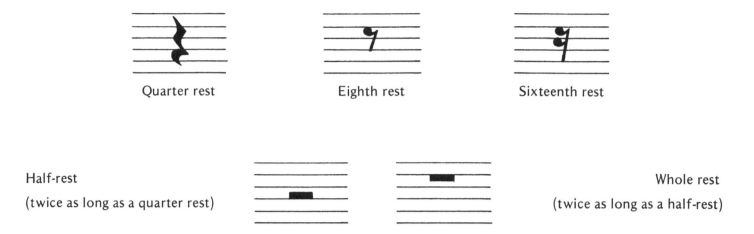

Quarter rest   Eighth rest   Sixteenth rest

Half-rest   Whole rest

(twice as long as a quarter rest)   (twice as long as a half-rest)

Occasionally an "H" or "P" or "CH" will appear in the tablature, indicating a "hammer-on," "pull-off" or "choke." These are left-hand techniques that will be described as they come up in the exercises.

THE BASICS

TUNING UP

Use a pitch pipe, tuning fork, piano or any instrument to give you a starting note. If you start with an E, you can locate all other notes on the guitar itself. Once you have tuned the 6th string to an E, fret it on the 5th fret as shown in illustration No. 2. This gives you an A, and you now can tune the 5th string to the A. Likewise, fret the 5th string on the 5th fret to get a D, and tune the 4th string to it . . . then continue as shown in illustration No. 3. When you fret a string, make sure your left hand does not touch any other string. Place your finger near the fret wire, but do not touch it.

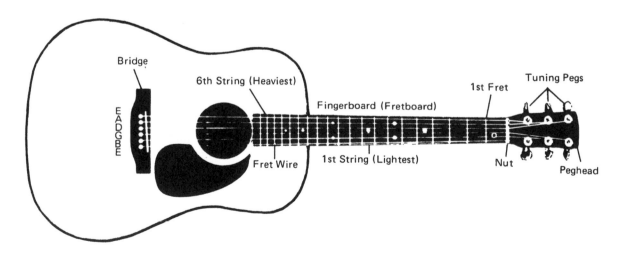

Illustration No. 1

6

Illustration No. 2

Illustration No. 3

Fretting the 6th string on the 5th fret.

If you start with a tuning fork (which usually gives you an A), tune the 5th string to it. Then fret the 6th string on the 5th fret and tune it till it sounds like the open A string. Then, finish tuning the other strings as before.

THE BASICS

THE CASSETTE TAPE AND HOW TO USE IT

The recording of all 37 exercises becomes a very valuable learning tool since the blues is "ear" music, developed and passed on from one "ear" musician to another. Most of the great blues guitarists, present and past, could not read a note. They learned by watching, listening and imitating other guitarists they admired. This is still the best way to learn the blues. Here's how to use this recording and book *together* in the same spirit:

First, read the text that precedes each exercise. It will describe some new scale, left hand technique, or chords with which you must practice to get comfortable.

Second, listen to the exercise. Listen to the use of the new techniques you've been practicing. Separate the lead and rhythm track on your stereo and hear each track separately.

Third, listen again while looking at the tablature. Don't try to play yet. There's little to be gained from memorizing tablature until you hear the music "in your mind."

Fourth, once the music is in your head, use the tablature to help you play. When you hear the music in your mind and search for it on your instrument, you're learning to play!

Finally, after learning to imitate the exercise, apply the new techniques in your own way while using the exercise as background. Tune out the lead channel, or play along with it, making up similar leads. Then go on to the next exercise.

The modern blues-guitar sounds of Eric Clapton, B.B. King and almost all blues and rock players grew out of the styles of rural black guitarists in the 20's and 30's, who used an unamplified guitar to accompany their singing. You can not play blues guitar with any authority unless you learn something about their styles.

EXERCISE NO. 1

Most of the early country-pickers played songs with a 12-bar form. You need only 3 chords to play a 12-bar blues: the tonic, subdominant and dominant, otherwise known as the 1st, 4th and 5th chords. (See the appendix on music theory if you're not familiar with these terms.)

Here are the three chords you will need for Exercise No. 1, a typical 12-bar blues.

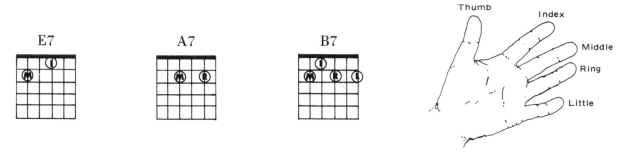

Learn these chords, and then play along with the 1st exercise. Notice that the guitar strums 4 times in each bar (measure), but sometimes it doubles up the first beat, resulting in this sound: bum- bum- bum- bum/ba-bum- bum- bum- bum/

EXERCISE NO. 1

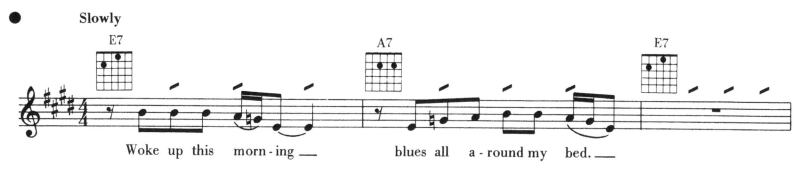

Woke up this morn-ing __ blues all a-round my bed. __

Woke up this morn-ing, __ blues all a-round my bed. __

Un-der-neath the blan - kets, ___

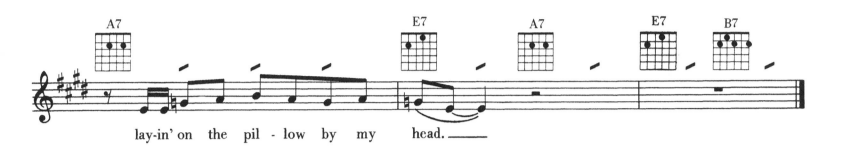

lay-in' on the pil - low by my head. _____

There are thousands of blues songs in this form. Once you learn the easy chords that follow, you can play the same progression in many different keys.

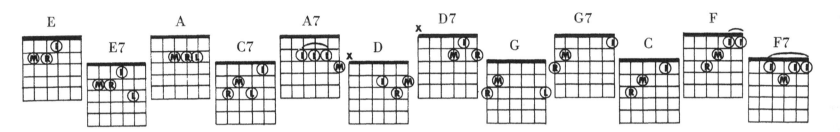

Now play through the following progressions. They're all in different keys, and they're all variations on the same 12-bar format. In spite of the slight differences between these progressions, you can sing the melody from Exercise No. 1 with all of them. Try it!

Key of G
| G ∕ ∕ ∕ | C7 ∕ ∕ ∕ | G ∕ ∕ ∕ | G7 ∕ ∕ ∕ | C7 ∕ ∕ ∕ | ∕ ∕ ∕ ∕ |
| G ∕ ∕ ∕ | ∕ ∕ ∕ ∕ | D7 ∕ ∕ ∕ | C7 ∕ ∕ ∕ | G ∕ ∕ ∕ | ∕ ∕ ∕ ∕ ‖

Key of C
| C ∕ ∕ ∕ | F7 ∕ ∕ ∕ | C ∕ ∕ ∕ | C7 ∕ ∕ ∕ | F ∕ ∕ ∕ | F7 ∕ ∕ ∕ |
| C ∕ ∕ ∕ | ∕ ∕ ∕ ∕ | G ∕ ∕ ∕ | G7 ∕ ∕ ∕ | C ∕ ∕ ∕ | ∕ ∕ ∕ ∕ ‖

Key of D
| D ∕ ∕ ∕ | D7 ∕ ∕ ∕ | D ∕ ∕ ∕ | D7 ∕ ∕ ∕ | G7 ∕ ∕ ∕ | ∕ ∕ ∕ ∕ |
| D7 ∕ ∕ ∕ | ∕ ∕ ∕ ∕ | A7 ∕ ∕ ∕ | G7 ∕ ∕ ∕ | D ∕ ∕ ∕ | A7 ∕ ∕ ∕ ‖

Key of A
| A7 ∕ ∕ ∕ | D7 ∕ ∕ ∕ | A ∕ ∕ ∕ | A7 ∕ ∕ ∕ | D ∕ ∕ ∕ | D7 ∕ ∕ ∕ |
| A7 ∕ ∕ ∕ | ∕ ∕ ∕ ∕ | E7 ∕ ∕ ∕ | D7 ∕ ∕ ∕ | A ∕ D7 ∕ | A7 ∕ E7 ∕ ‖

In Exercise No. 2 (another blues in E), you make use of the D7 and A7 chords in a new way. Sometimes you slide up to a chord from one fret back, like this.

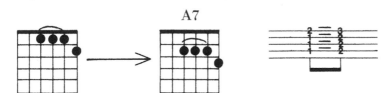

(Here's how the slide looks in the tablature. Lines connecting notes indicate sliding.)

Sometimes you move a chord up a few frets to get a new chord:

A7 moved up two frets becomes B7   D7 moved up two frets becomes E7

Study the new uses of chord formations in Exercise No. 2 and learn the guitar part.

EXERCISE NO. 2

Good morn-in' blues,_____ what can I do for you?_____

It's been a long, long time,_____

I thought I'd seen the last of you.

The third exercise uses the same techniques, in the key of A. Now the right hand has added something new: the thumb keeps thumping away on a bass string (the 5th, or A string) while the fingers pick the chords out on the higher strings.

—————————————EXERCISE NO. 3

I did some drink-in', ___   and lost my   head,_ you know my   pock-et's emp-ty and my

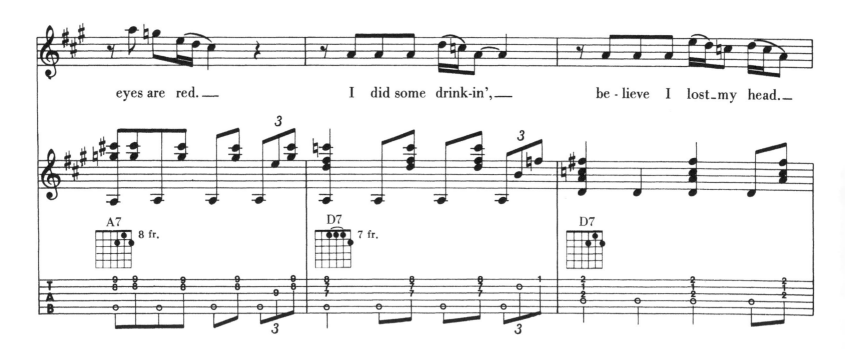

eyes are red.___   I did some drink-in',___   be-lieve I lost_my head._

I went look-ing for my wom-an,

brought the blues home in - stead.

The diagram that follows shows the notes in a blues scale for the key of E. These are not the only notes that can be played in an 'E blues' but they make a good starting point, so play them over and over, using the suggested fingering. When they're familiar to you, try the 4th exercise. In this example, your thumb thumps out the bass notes, as before, and your fingers pick out the melody notes from the blues scale…meanwhile, you're playing those A7 and D7 chords up the neck.

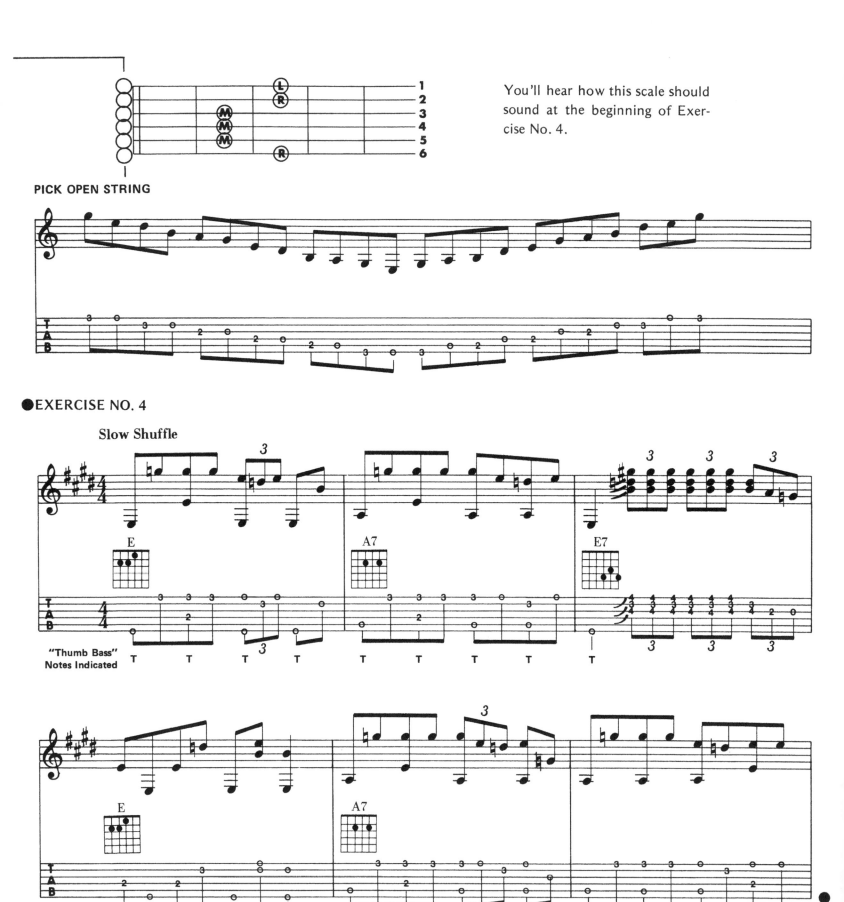

You'll hear how this scale should sound at the beginning of Exercise No. 4.

PICK OPEN STRING

● **EXERCISE NO. 4**

Slow Shuffle

"Thumb Bass"
Notes Indicated

The last country-blues exercise, number 5, combines everything we've done so far and adds three new techniques. The first is a bass line played on the E and A chords. You don't need to play the entire chord to get this effect—only one string is fretted.

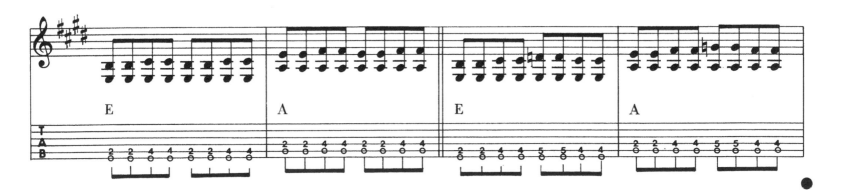

The second new technique—"choking" or stretching a string with your left hand, after you pick it. The illustrations below show how the left hand looks "choking" a string.

Before   . . . and

After choking
a string

How choking a string looks in tablature:

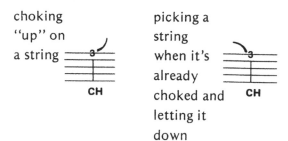

choking "up" on a string

picking a string when it's already choked and letting it down

The third new technique is a trill—three notes played together, rapid-fire. First you pick a string, then hammer onto it a few frets higher (sounding the note by striking the string on the fret with your left hand), then pull off rapidly with your left hand, sounding the third note. It looks like this in tablature:

Each of these techniques is demonstrated on the tape, just before Exercise No. 5.

EXERCISE NO. 5

Slowly

Good morn-in' blues, _____ hope you don't plan _ to stay too

long. _____

Good morn - in' blues, _____

E   7FR   E7   HP   A

CH   CH   CH   CH

hope you don't plan to stay too   long. _____

I'm go - in'

E7

CH CH CH

out   to   find that wom-an, _____

don't you be here when I come

B7   A

home. —

CH   CH

E

B7

E7

H

COUNTRY BLUES DISCOGRAPHY

After each chapter, I list several masters of the style you've just studied. Listen to their records to learn more tunes and more picking ideas built around the techniques in these exercises. Once you can really play the exercises, you'll find you can play countless tunes by these artists. Records go in and out of print, so I'm not naming specific discs, but any big record store carries examples of the work of these bluesmen.

Big Bill Broonzy, Big Joe Williams, Brownie McGhee, Robert Johnson, Scrapper Blackwell — their records are solid source material. Fancy finger-picking stylists include Furry Lewis, Mance Lipscomb and Mississippi John Hurt.

John Lee Hooker and Lightnin' Hopkins are masters of the style, but look for recordings on which they play without accompaniment. (Today they use electric back-up, although their style has not changed much.)

Most of the players keep a constant bass-note accompaniment pulsing through all their tunes. It's an essential part of the style — it gives the solo guitarist his own back-up. To master this technique, (in Exercise Nos. 3, 4 and 5) start by singing tunes and accompanying yourself only with the thumping bass and the necessary chord changes. When your thumb does this automatically, then add whatever fill-in notes you can by picking the high strings with your fingers. Make the thumb-bass notes the foundation of the music.

In the rock music of the 50's and early 60's, almost every guitar break sounded like an imitation of Chuck Berry. His style bridges country blues and modern blues sounds. Therefore, we will examine a lot of Chuck Berry licks. Not only will they help you get a handle on more contemporary styles, they will provide a lot of fun in themselves.

To achieve a cleaner, sharper attack with this style of music, use a flat-pick. Such picks come in many shapes, sizes and thicknesses, but it's best to start with a "medium" (rather than light or heavy) pick in one of the illustrated shapes. The illustration below shows how to hold the pick.

Generally, you pick down on the downbeat and up on the upbeat. For the rock rhythms in this chapter, you will use almost all downstrokes!

Now, you need a few new chords and some fingerboard theory. Look at the fingerboard chart below. It tells you where the notes are located on the 5th and 6th strings.

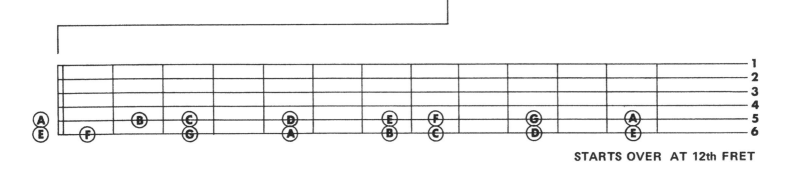

STARTS OVER AT 12th FRET

Now, look at the A chord pictured on the following page, with two "extensions." The chord root is the 6th string; check the fingerboard chart and you'll see that the 6th string on the 5th fret is, sure enough, an A. If you move the chord up to the 7th fret it becomes a B chord (the 6th string on the 7th fret is B). In the "extensions," the little finger has to extend itself quite a way up. Practice with the bit of music below and move to different places on the neck, always thinking about which chord you're playing (a G on the 3rd fret, a C on the 8th, and so on).

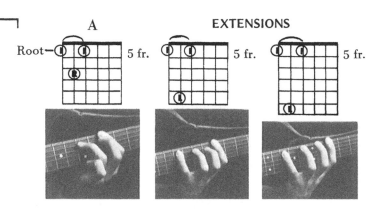

A — EXTENSIONS

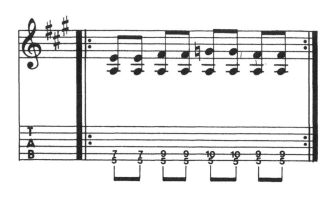

The D chord below, with its two "extensions," is like the A chord you just learned, but your left hand moves "down a string" so that the 5th string becomes the root. (As you see on the fingerboard chart, the 5th string on the 5th fret is an D.)

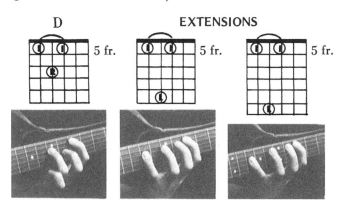

D — EXTENSIONS

Once you've learned the A pattern and D pattern, listen to Exercise No. 6 and learn the back-up guitar part.

(A NOTE ABOUT 12/8 TIME: think of it as 4 beats to a measure, 3 eighth notes per beat: 111 222 333 444. Since three eighth notes make one beat, a single beat might look like this: ♪♪♪

or this: ♩ ♪

or this: ♩.

or this: ♪.

EXERCISE NO. 6
(RHYTHM)
Moderately Slow Shuffle

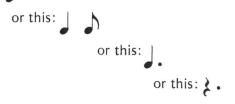

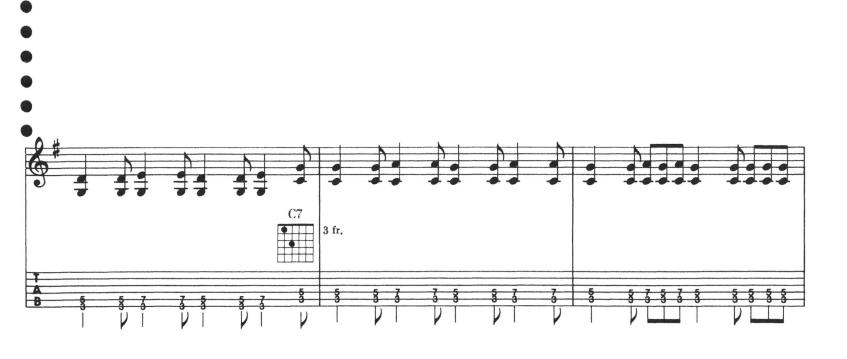

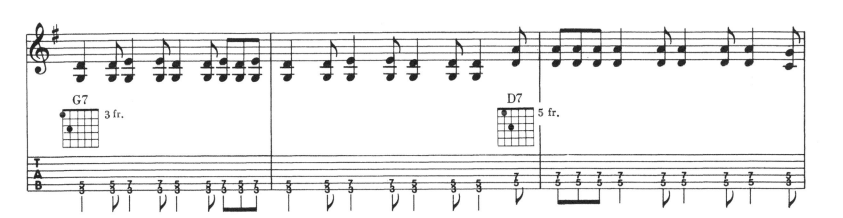

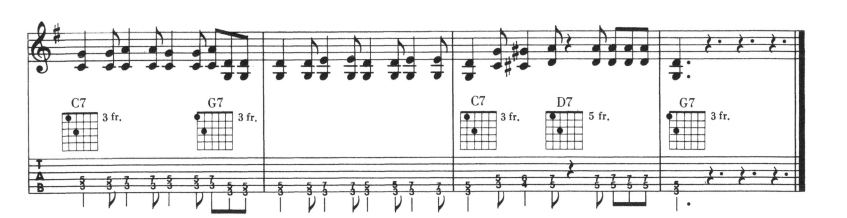

The fingerboard chart below shows you pairs of notes with which you must become familiar to play this style of lead guitar. The notes cluster mostly around the F or Fm chord; therefore, assume the F or Fm position when you play these licks. Try playing the line of music below that uses these pairs of notes.

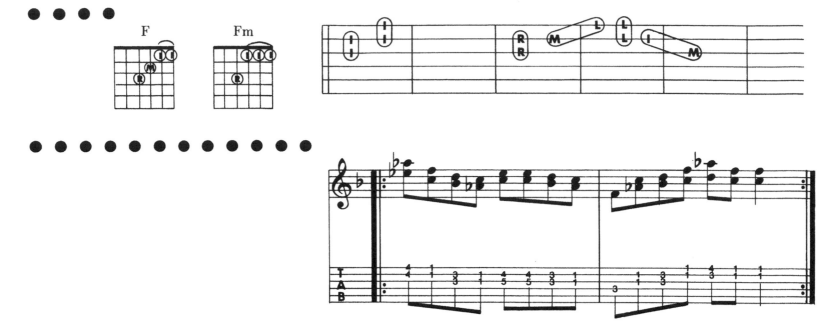

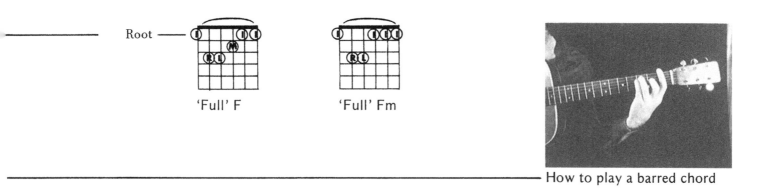

You can play this set of licks in any key, by moving your starting chord (the F or Fm position) up the neck. This is easy to do once you learn the fingerboard chart on page 19. For example , if you move a full F or Fm chord up two frets it becomes a G (the 6th string on the 3rd fret is G); if you play that set of licks starting from this new position you're in the key of G.

Root ——

'Full' F   'Full' Fm

How to play a barred chord

Incidentally, don't bother to use a barred-chord as a "starting place". The 1st string is the same note as the 6th string in an F chord, so you can use the partial F chord to get "in position" and consider the 1st string the root.

EXERCISE NO. 6 is in G; start with your left hand in the F position on the 3rd fret.

● (Note: When you slide up to a note from one or two frets back,
    it looks like this in tablature: ═╪═ Or this: ═╤═ Pick the
                                     6   6 note on the
                                               6th fret &
    Pick the note on the 4th or 5th   slide down
    fret and quickly slide up to the 6th fret.)   a few frets.

EXERCISE NO.6 (LEAD)

Moderately Slow Shuffle

The next exercise uses the same licks in more of a rock 'n' roll context. Now you're in C; start with the F or Fm position at the 8th fret.

_____EXERCISE NO. 7 (RHYTHM)

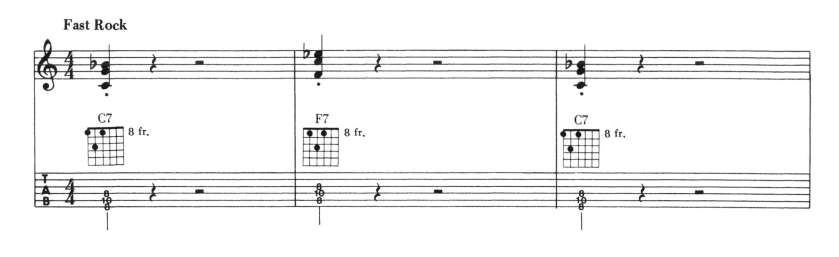

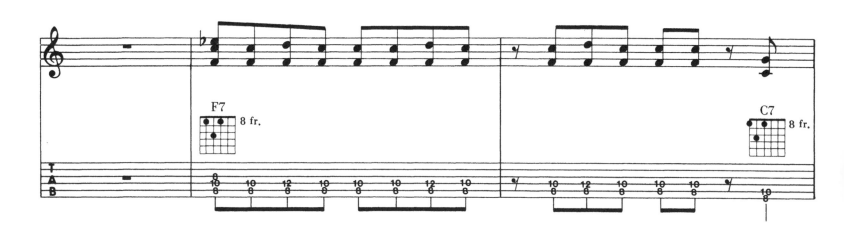

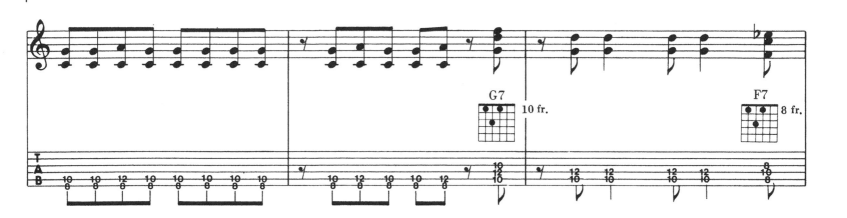

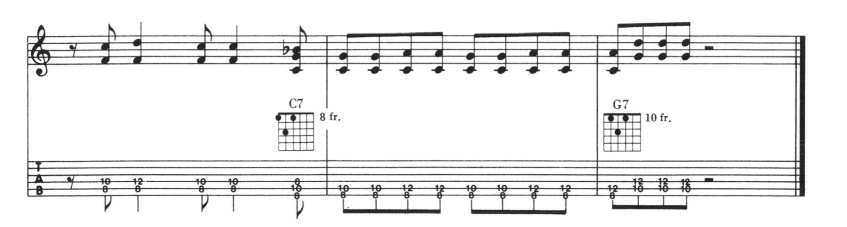

EXERCISE NO. 7 (LEAD)

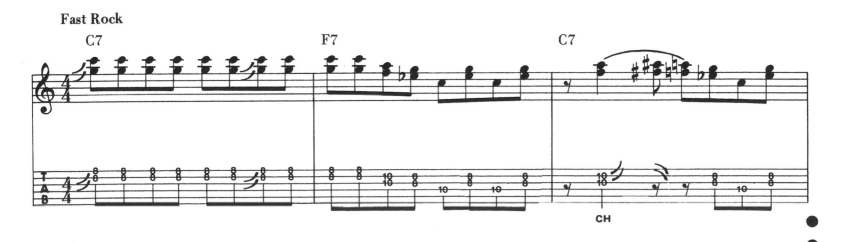

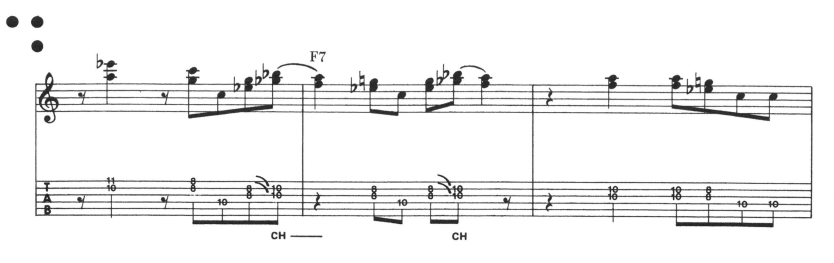

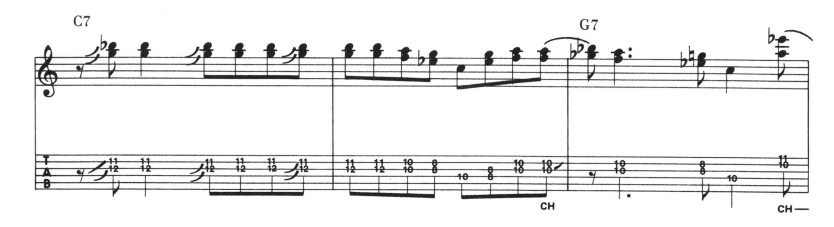

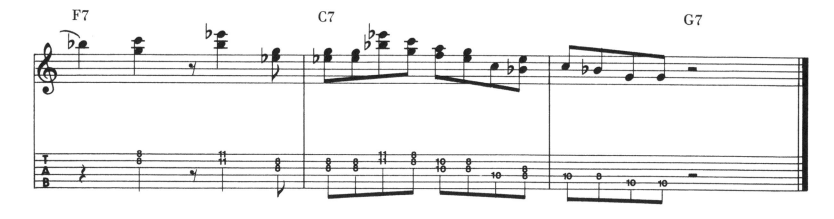

The last exercise in this style is in A. To get a shuffle beat rhythm, the back-up guitar alternates up and down strokes, giving emphasis to the downbeat.

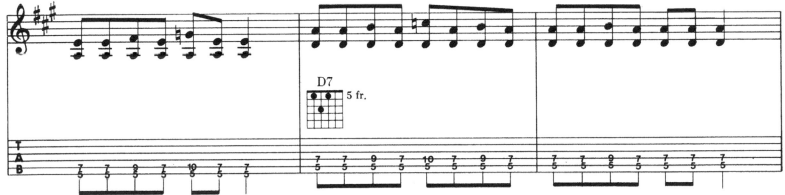

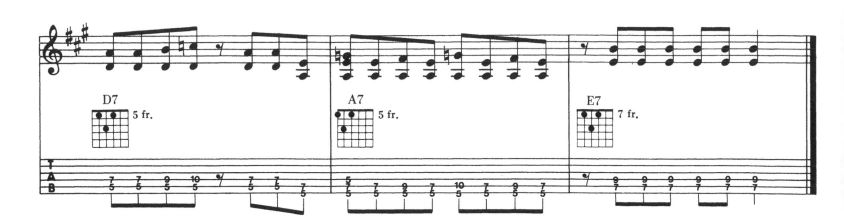

EXERCISE NO. 8 (LEAD)

Fast Shuffle

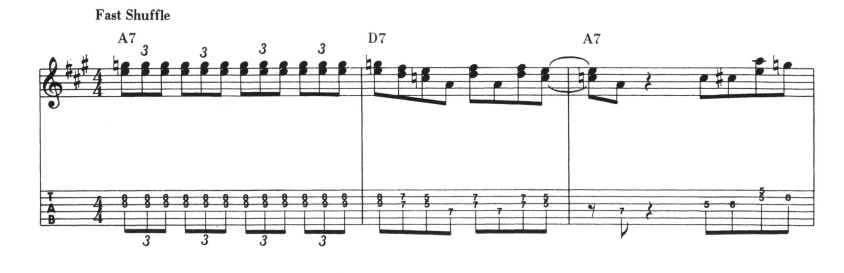

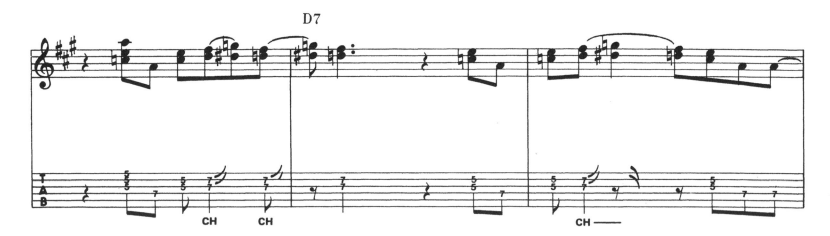

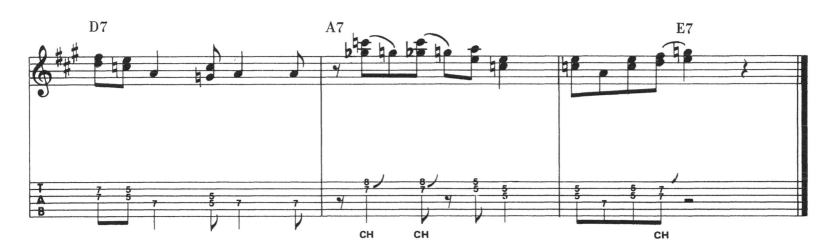

Before you go to the modern blues and rock exercises, go back and play your own improvised leads over the preceding three tunes. Get out the tape accompanying this book — tune out the lead guitar and use the rhythm track for practice. It's the next best thing to playing with other people.

CHUCK BERRY-STYLE BLUES DISCOGRAPHY

Naturally, listen to Chuck Berry first–old or new records. Any of the guitarists of the early 60's and late 50's will give you more ideas along the same lines. Listen to the lead guitar on Elvis Presley's early music (it's often Scotty Moore). Likewise, listen to Buddy Holly & The Crickets, The Beach Boys' early records, The Ventures, Dick Dale, Bo Diddley. On early Beatles and Rolling Stones records, you'll hear George Harrison and Keith Richard imitating Chuck Berry licks, note-for-note. You'll also hear the back-up style (taught in this chapter) now being used in contemporary rock. Blues bands, in the 50's and 60's, used these same back-up techniques.

THE BLUES SCALE —— 1st POSITION

The scale shown on the fingerboard below is the first in a series of moveable blues scales with which you'll be working. They'll all be introduced in the key of G, but you will use them in all keys. As I said when I showed you the E scale, these are not the only notes you'll play in a G blues, but they make a good starting point.

Set your left hand in the F or F minor position to practice this scale (I use the partial F chord, as in the Chuck Berry licks) and practice the scale over and over.

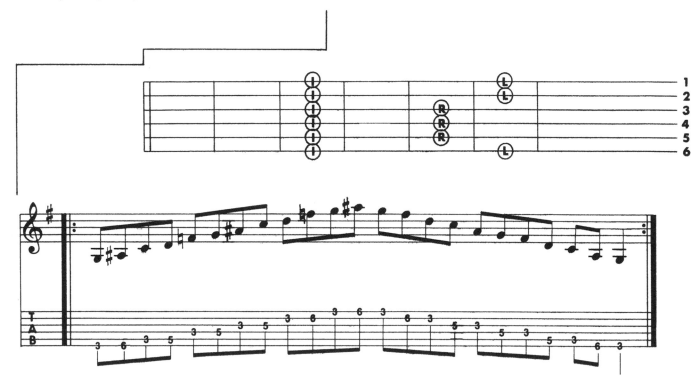

Now try Exercise No. 9. The back-up part is the same as in No. 6 and the lead is built off this 1st position scale.

EXERCISE NO. 9 (LEAD)

Moderately Slow Shuffle

The next exercise is a medium-tempo, shuffle-beat blues, using the same techniques as Exercise No. 9, transposed up a step. Set your left hand in the F position on the 5th fret and play the 1st position scale; this puts you in the key of A. The rhythm part is the same as in No. 8.

Fast Shuffle

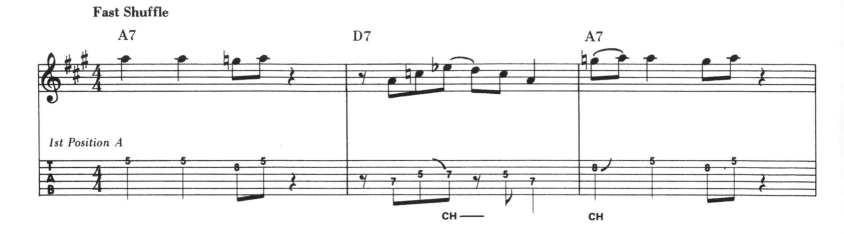

1st Position A

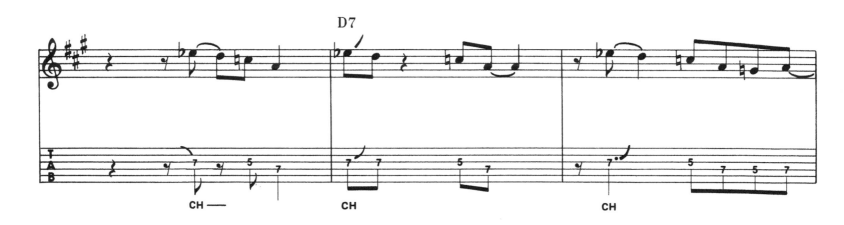

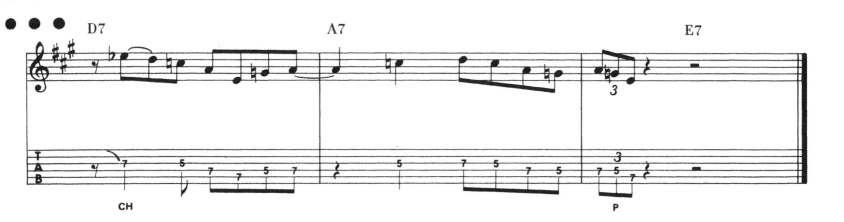

D7   A7   E7

CH   P

The next exercise is in C; therefore, move the first position scale up to the 8th fret. Notice that the lead part contains notes that are not in the scale, but around it. A left-hand, vibrato technique is used here, also, which is achieved by choking a string up and down rapidly to sustain a note. It takes some doing to get this effect, so don't be discouraged when it does not come off right away.

The choke, with vibrato, looks like this in tablature:

EXERCISE NO. 11 (RHYTHM)

Fast Shuffle

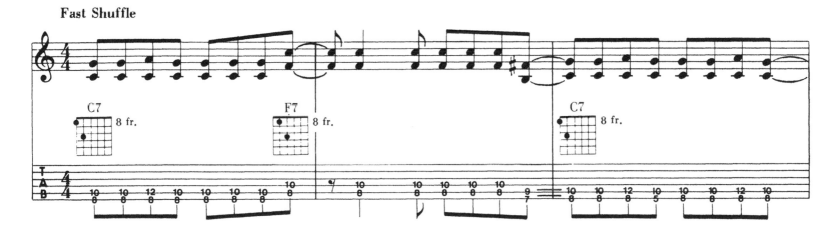

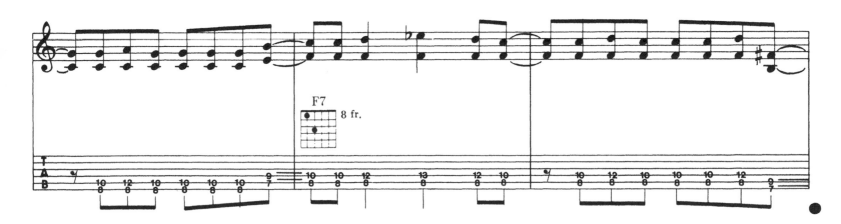

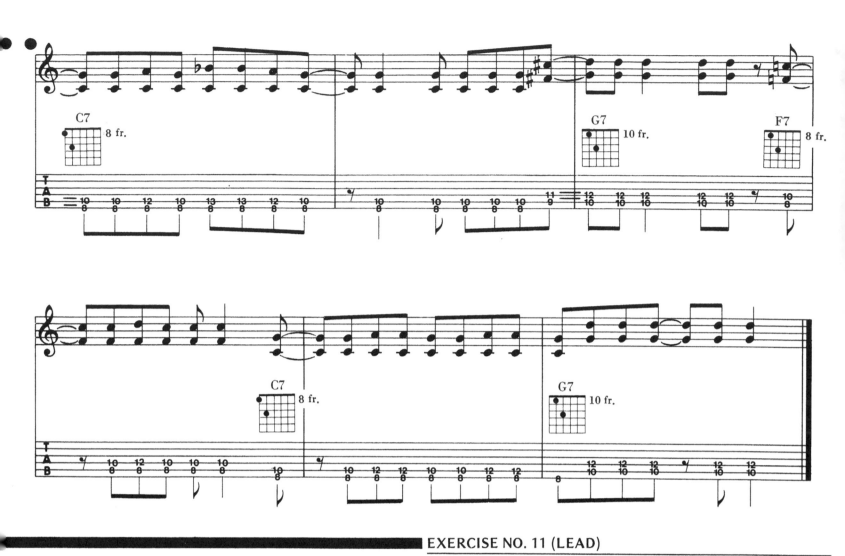

EXERCISE NO. 11 (LEAD)

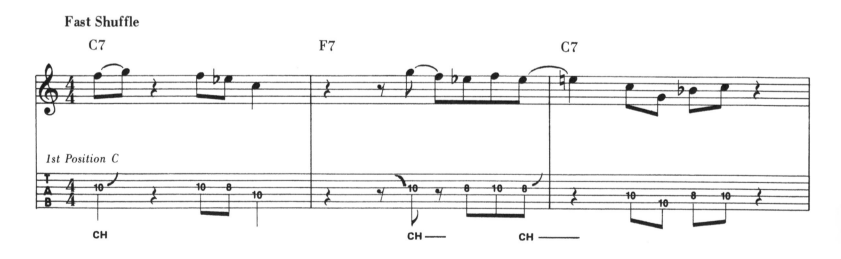

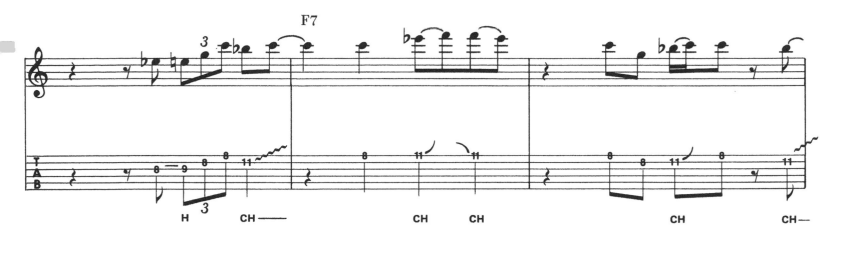

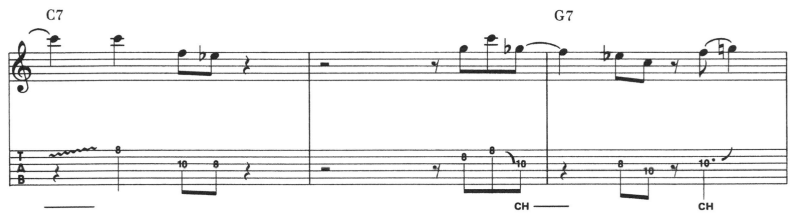

You've now used the first-position blues-scale to play three 12-bar progressions in three different keys. Before you go ahead to learn the 2nd position, use the 1st scale in some improvisations of your own. Tune out the lead track on the accompanying recording and play against the back-up. If you can get a guitarist or pianist to play back-up for you so much the better. Remember when you make up lead lines, simplicity and repetition will sound great and will make your practice easier. One good lick, repeated several times in a tune, can give your playing continuity. Notice the empty space in the examples ... the times you do not play add interest to the music and give you breathing space.

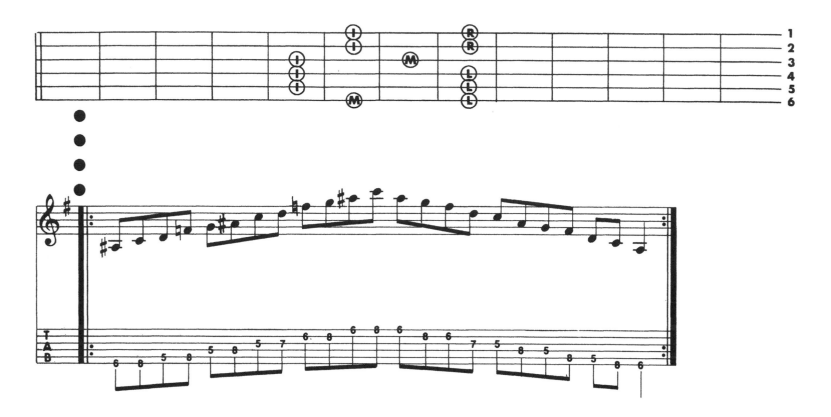

To get your left hand set for this position, move the F position up three frets (to the 6th fret—notice the F formation there in the fretboard chart). You can also relate the 2nd position to the "Chuck Berry" style by moving up to the 6th and 7th frets (on the 2nd and 3rd strings).

Play this scale for a while, then use Exercise No. 12.

EXERCISE NO.12 (LEAD)

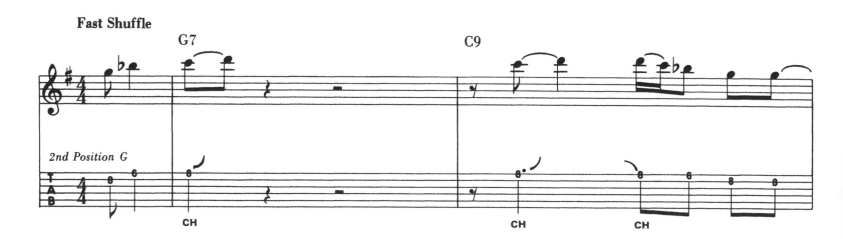

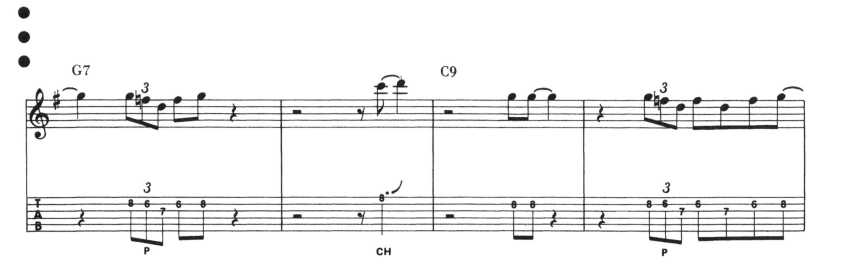

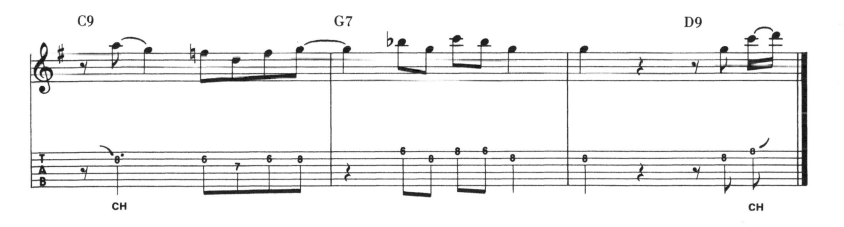

The back-up in this exercise uses two new chords:

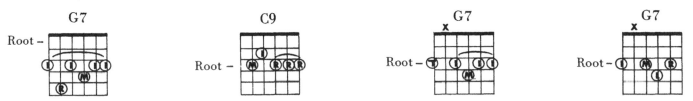

Note that you have three alternative ways to play G7, all with the root in the 6th string. The D9, in the 12th exercise, is the C9 chord moved up two frets.

Fast Shuffle

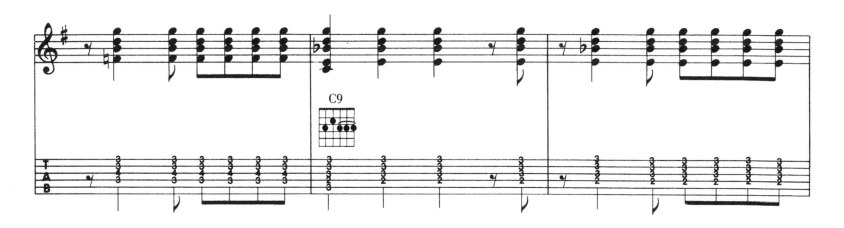

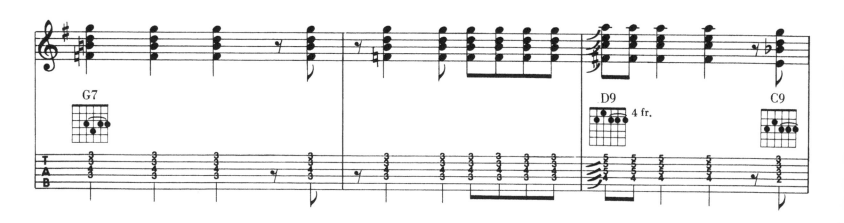

In the following exercise the lead guitar moves back and forth in the 1st and 2nd positions. The key is F; hence, your left hand will play two frets below the G position. The rock feeling here is quite different from the Chuck Berry style.

■■■■■■■■■EXERCISE NO. 13 (LEAD)

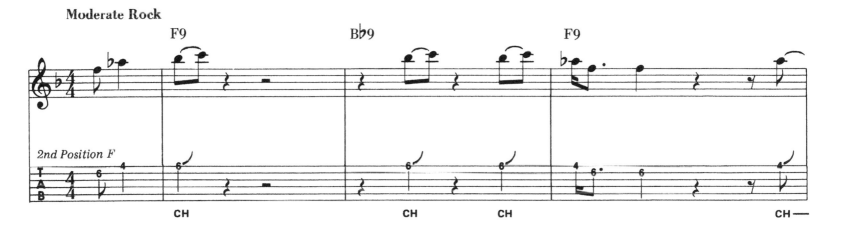

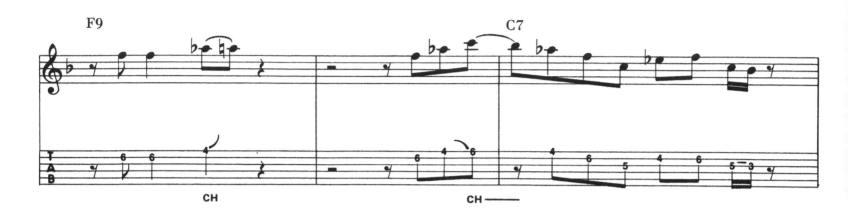

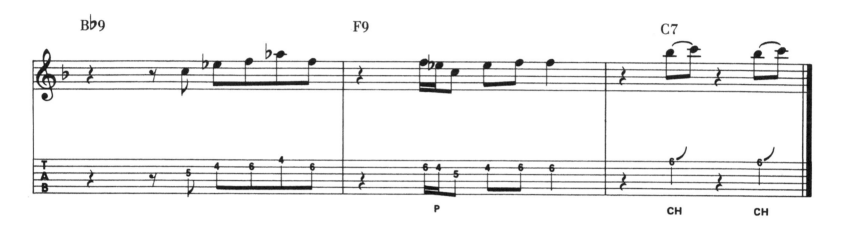

The new chord position in this back-up part (the Bb9) is the same as the G7 in the last exercise, only a ninth is added on the 1st string.

Here are two ways to play the chord:

All three of the chords used in this back-up part have a high C on top in the first string, which adds an attractive consistency to the part.

● ● ● ● ● ● **EXERCISE NO. 13 (RHYTHM)** ● ● ● ● ● ● ● ●

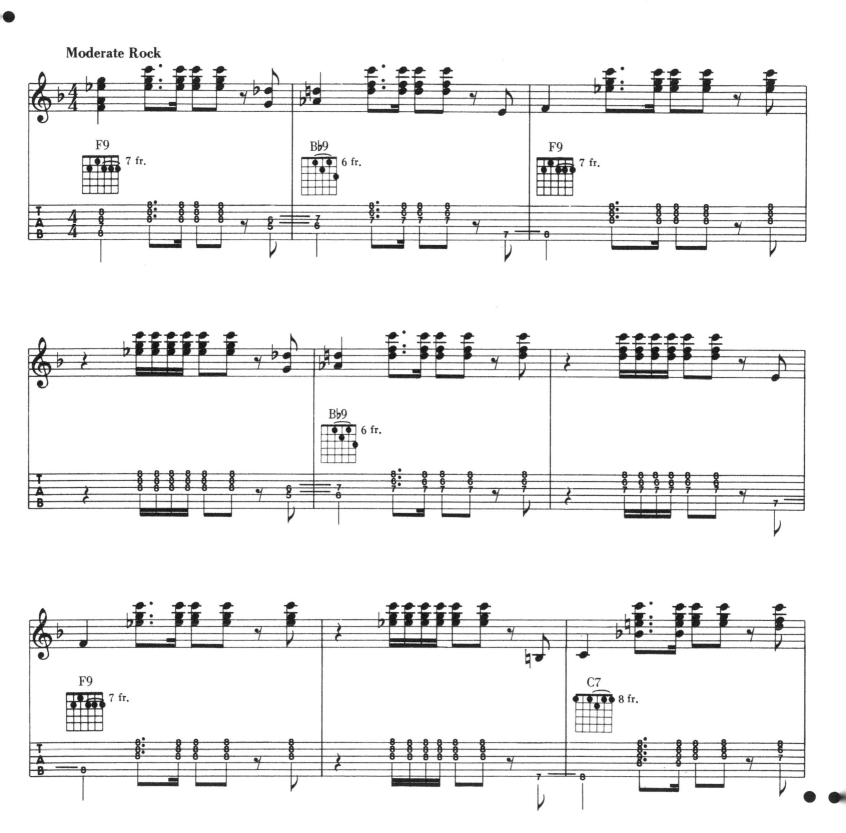

A blues tune often begins on a "turn-around," usually the last four measures of the 12-bar progression. Exercise No. 14 is an example of this kind of introduction. The exercise is in Bb.

EXERCISE NO. 14 (LEAD)

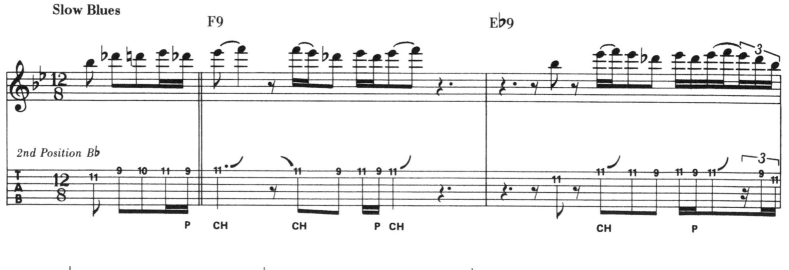

The slides you hear on the F9 and Eb9 chords (in the back-up) are played only on the first three strings, as shown in the diagram:

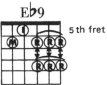

EXERCISE NO. 14 (RHYTHM)

3rd POSITION BLUES SCALE

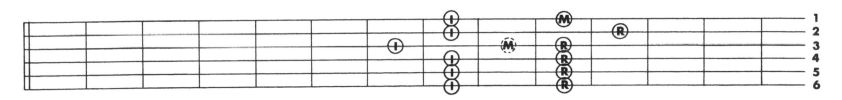

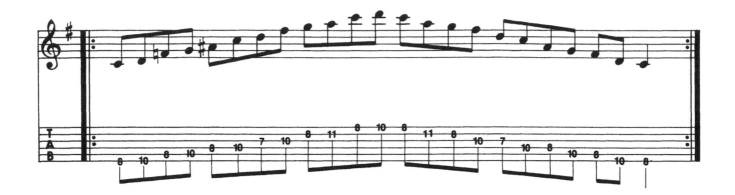

The "ghost note" on the 3rd string, besides being an often-played note in this scale, is part of a device you can use to get your left hand set for the 3rd position. It's part of an F formation that starts on the 8th fret—a C chord, in other words.

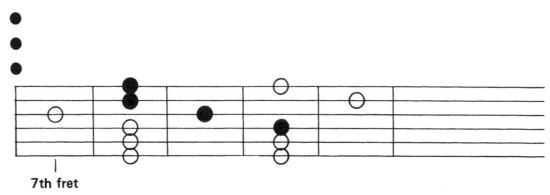

7th fret

When you were getting set for the 1st position, you played an F formation on the 3rd fret—a G chord. For the 3rd position, jump up 5 frets higher.

When you are asked to play a chord formation "five frets higher," remember that this means exactly the same thing as "playing the 4 chord" or "playing the subdominant." (See the music theory appendix at the end of the book.)

To find the 3rd position, follow this rule: Play the tonic in the F formation! Move the F formation to the subdominant, which is "five frets higher." Example: In the key of F, play an F formation on the first fret (the tonic). Then, move the F formation "five frets higher" to the subdominant (Bb). Now your hand is set for 3rd position scales.

● **EXERCISE NO. 15 (LEAD)**

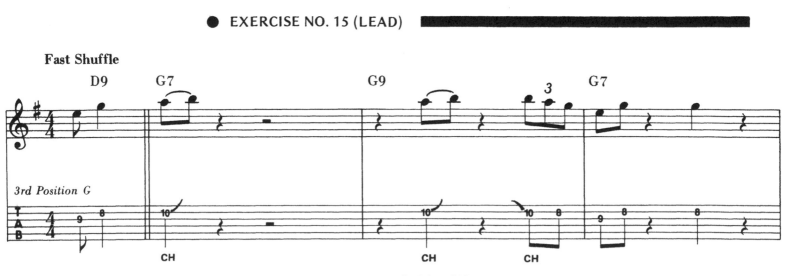

EXERCISE NO. 15 (RHYTHM)

There's a new G9 chord in the back-up part to this exercise, and you can slide up on its top three strings, as illustrated. Note that you don't play the root of this chord.

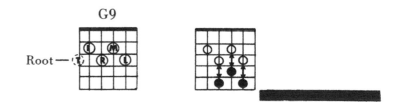

EXERCISE NO. 15
RHYTHM

Fast Shuffle

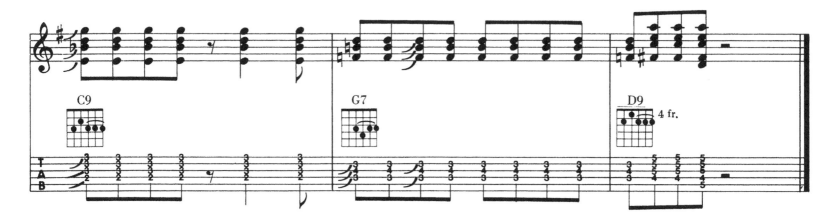

Here's a blues in A played up around the 3rd position. This is a new 8-bar blues; it's not heard as often as the 12-bar blues, but it is the progression for many popular blues tunes.

EXERCISE NO. 16 (LEAD)

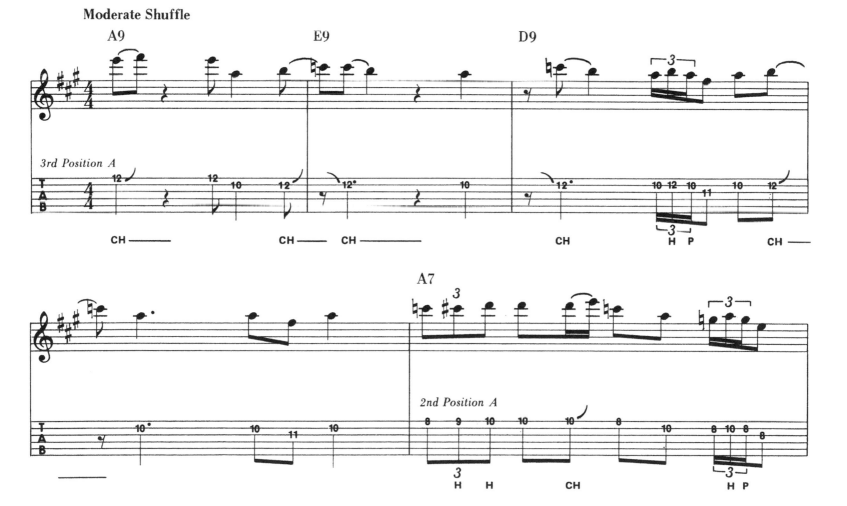

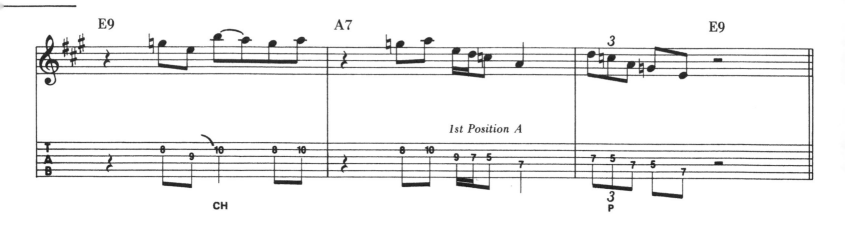

EXERCISE NO. 16 (RHYTHM)

Moderate Shuffle

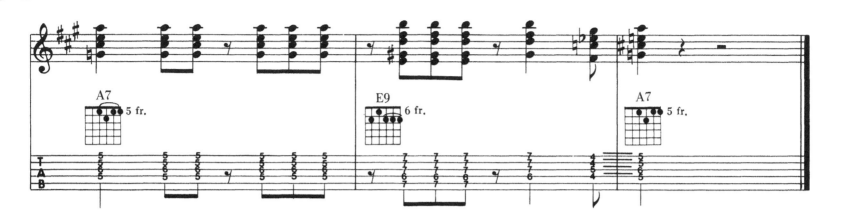

4th POSITION BLUES SCALE

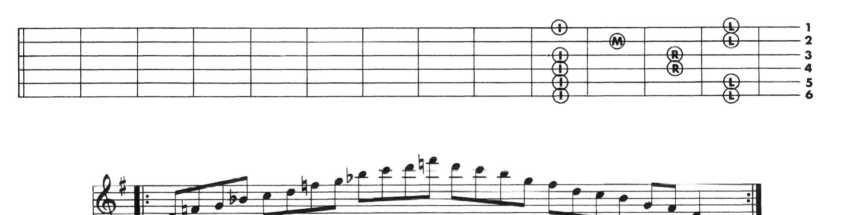

Example No. 17 is a rock blues in a minor key. All the positions you've been learning will work for minor or major blues. This one is played out of the 4th position. Here are the minor chords you'll need for the back-up (the minor and minor-seventh chords are interchangeable):

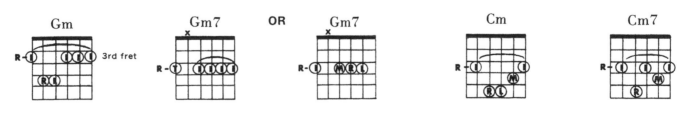

The Dm and Dm7 are, of course, the same as Cm and Cm7, moved up two frets. Notice how the back-up guitar slides up two frets on these minor chords for embellishment. You can slide on the whole chord or on just a few strings.

EXERCISE NO. 17 (RHYTHM)

Moderate Rock

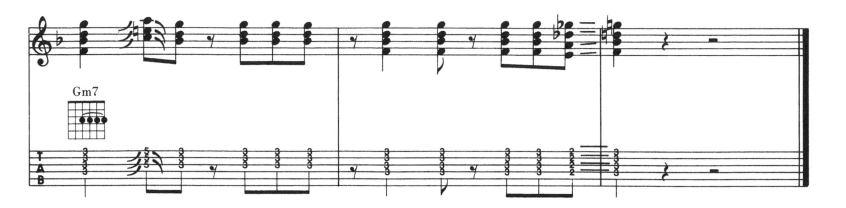

EXERCISE NO. 17 (LEAD)

Moderate Rock

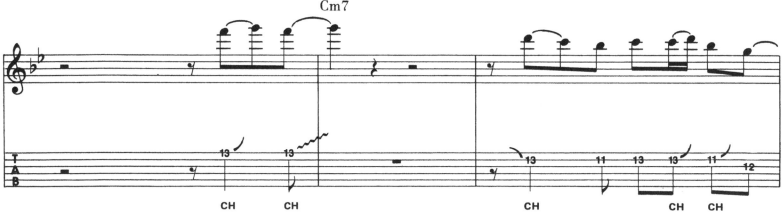

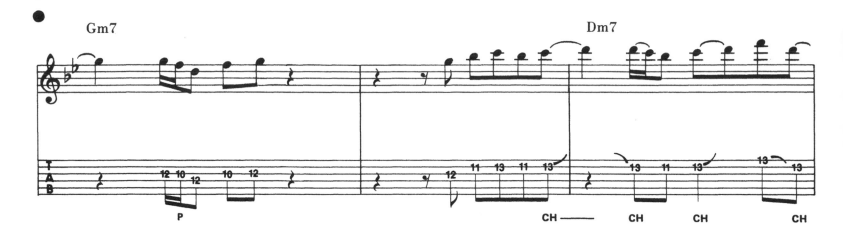

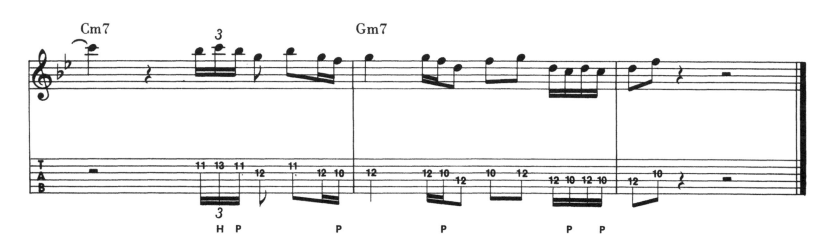

5th POSITION BLUES SCALE

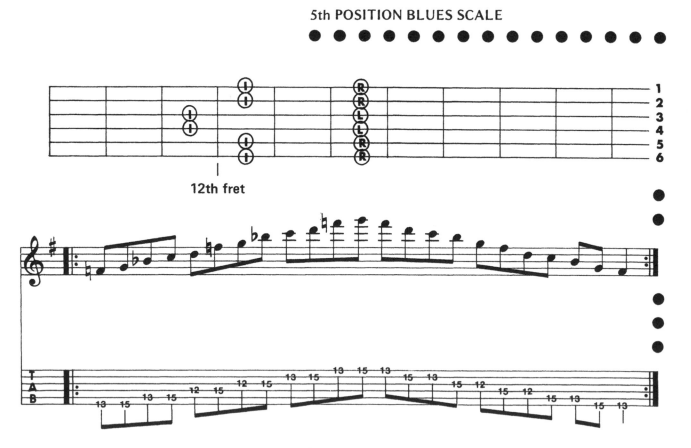

12th fret

52

● Exercise No. 18 is another minor blues. The lead guitar uses 4th and 5th position scales.
— Now that you're becoming familiar with minor chords, note that there is a minor chord contained in the 1st position scale, and another in the 4th position. To play Exercise No. 18, which is in Dm, play a Dm on the 5th fret, and you'll be set for the 4th position. This would work as well if the key were D major.

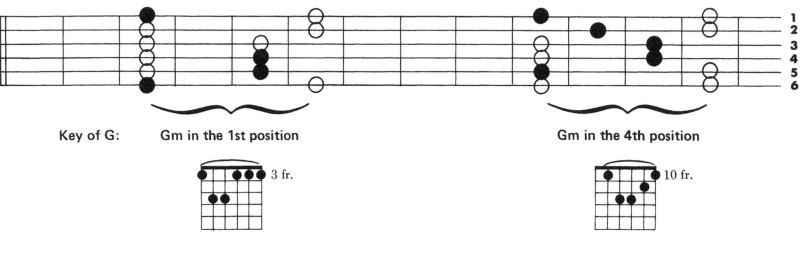

Key of G: Gm in the 1st position   Gm in the 4th position

EXERCISE NO. 18 (RHYTHM)

Slow Blues

Slow Blues

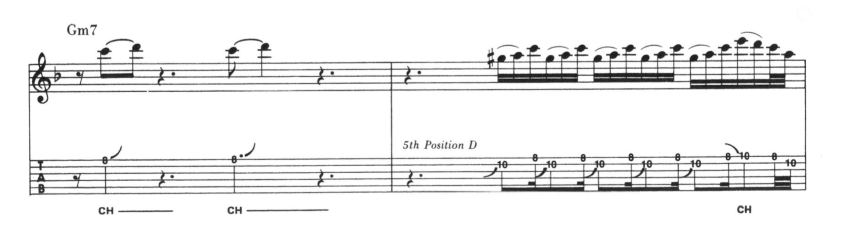

Here's another 8-bar blues, like No. 16; it's a variation of the 8-bar progression. The lead guitar uses 4th and 5th position scales.

EXERCISE NO. 19 (RHYTHM)

Slow Blues

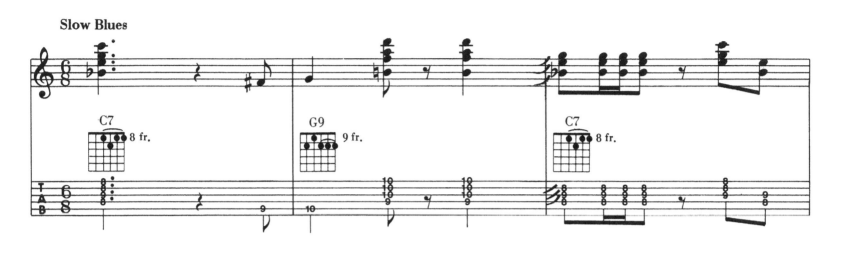

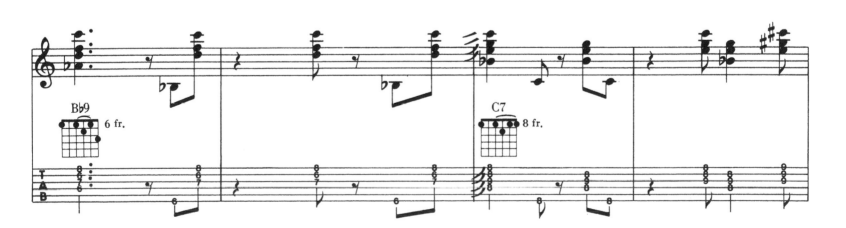

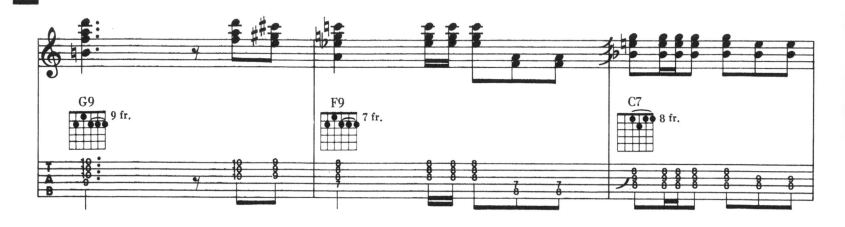

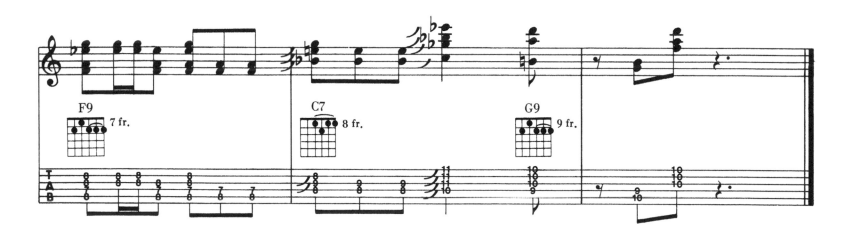

EXERCISE NO. 19 (LEAD)

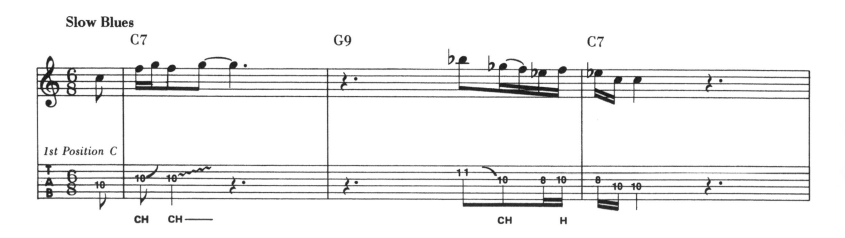

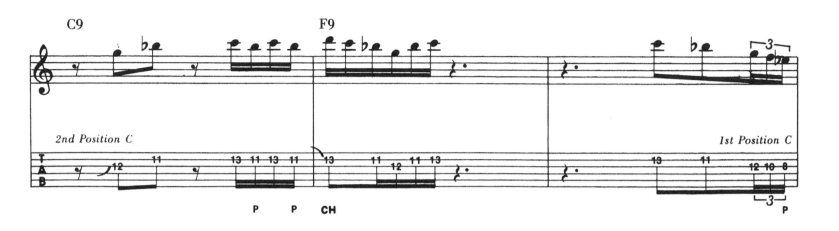

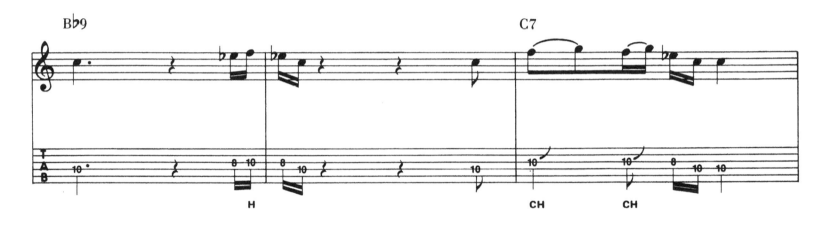

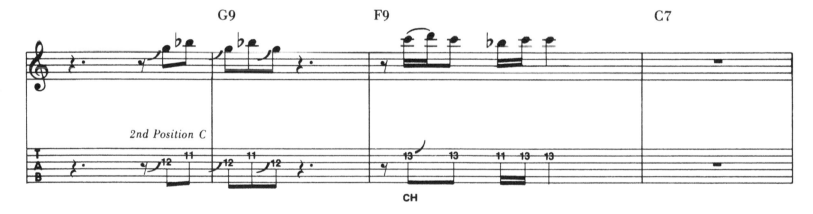

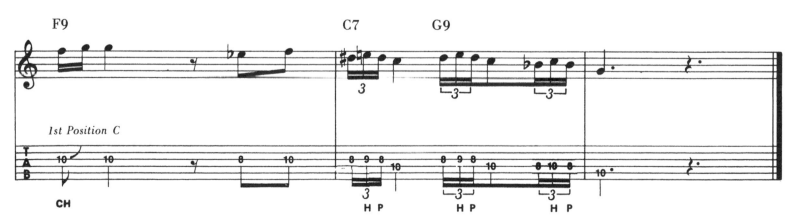

Now that you've worked with all 5 of these blues scales, go back and use the rhythm tracks from the tape to practice; make up your own lead parts. Naturally, you can use any position to play lead for any of these exercises.

MODERN BLUES STYLES — DISCOGRAPHY

As you can tell from the recording, the exercises and scales in this chapter work in many different blues formats. Just about any blues records from the last fifteen years will provide you with similar examples of blues guitar playing.

B.B. King is the ultimate source of modern blues guitar. He inspired countless guitarists—most of the young contemporary blues players. Listen to any of his records. Albert King (no relation to B.B.), Buddy Guy, T-Bone Walker and Earl Hooker are urban guitarists who play dynamite blues. Eric Clapton's records with John Mayall and the Bluesbreakers and Bloomfield's work with the Butterfield Blues Band are 100% blues. Their later pop music records have much less guitar playing.

You can learn many tunes and hear occasional guitar licks from the recordings of these other notable modern bluesmen: Howling Wolf, Junior Wells, Paul Butterfield, Little Walter, Jimmy Reed, Otis Rush. They all were blues stars of the 50's and 60's and many of them are still playing.

The blues scales you've been learning will work perfectly in most R&B, rock and country tunes. In fact, most rock and R&B lead guitarists are simply playing blues lines over different progressions. In Exercise No. 20, "House Of The Rising Sun," the lead guitar plays blues licks in the first few positions (in the key of A), even though the chord progression moves around quite a bit.

EXERCISE NO. 20 (LEAD)

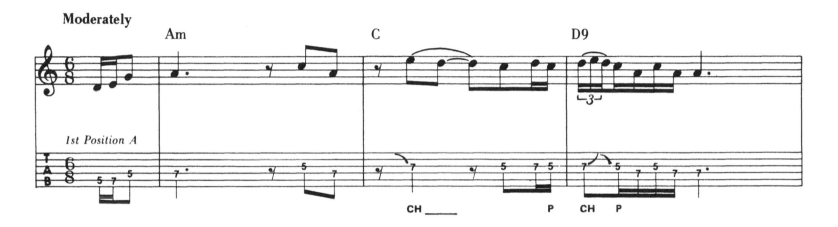

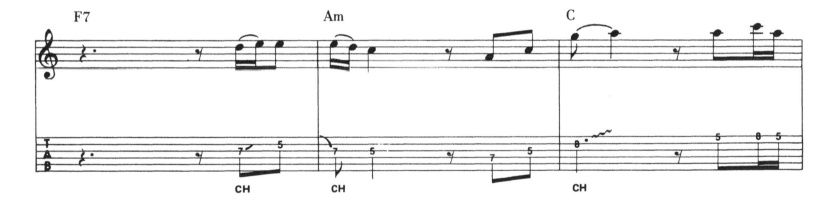

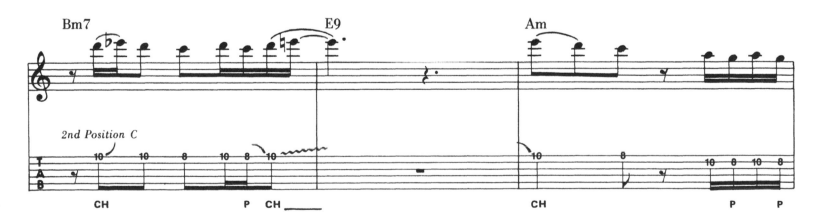

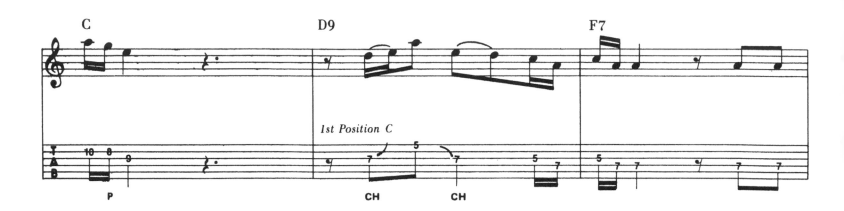

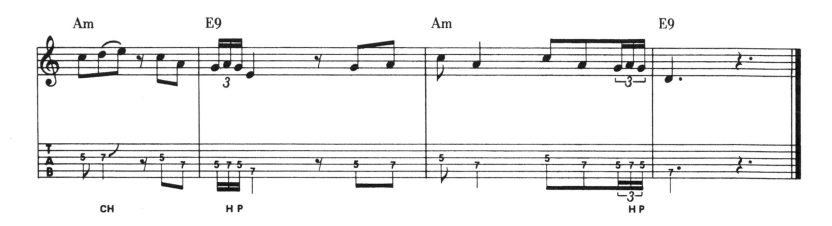

Exercise No. 21 is another typical rock progression, in the key of A. Again, the lead guitar plays A blues scales.

EXERCISE NO. 21 (LEAD)

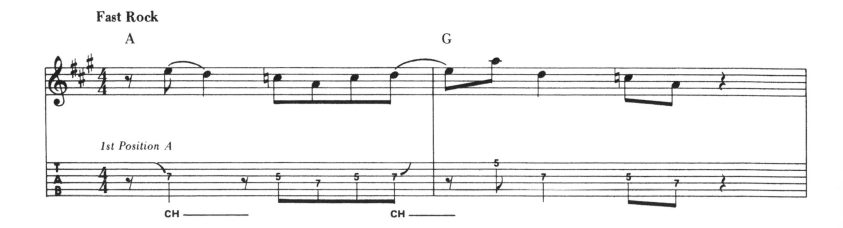

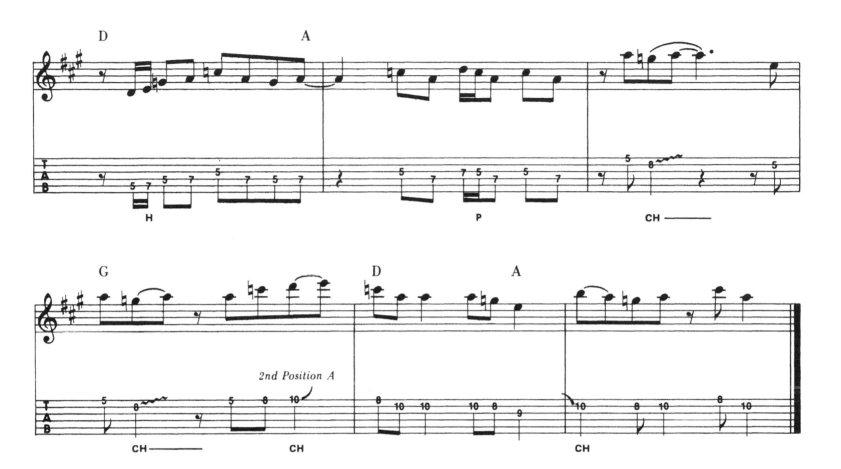

If a tune doesn't lend itself to bluesy licks and needs more "major" and less "minor" sounds, you can often play blues licks a 6th above the song's key. This is the same as going to the relative minor, and playing scales out of that key. (See the Music Theory Appendix for more information on how to find the relative minor, and how to "move up a 6th.") For example, in Exercise No. 22, in the key of C, the lead guitar plays 1st and 2nd position blues licks in A—because A is a 6th above C.

EXERCISE NO. 22 (LEAD)

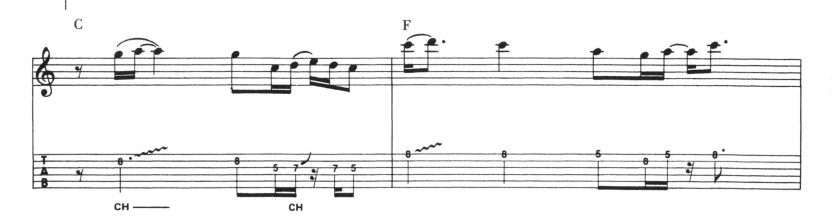

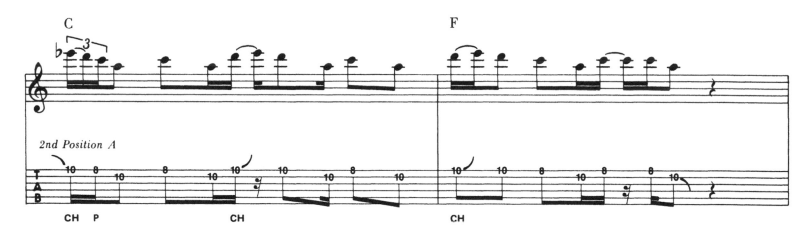

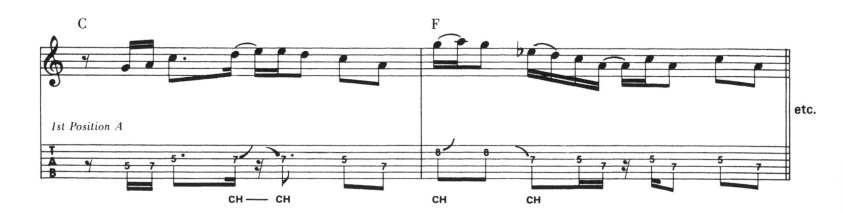

etc.

Now play a few bars of C blues scales over the same rhythm part (as in Exercise No. 23) and hear how different it sounds.

EXERCISE NO. 23 (LEAD) ●

Funky Rock Beat

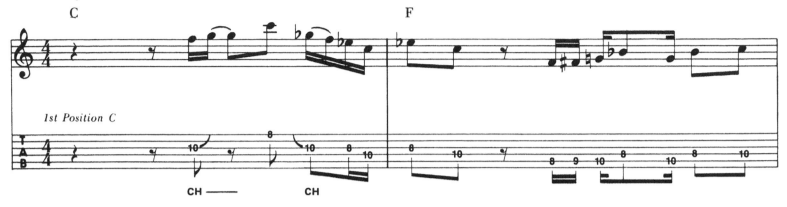

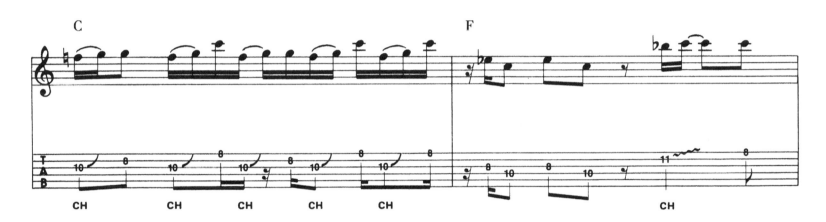

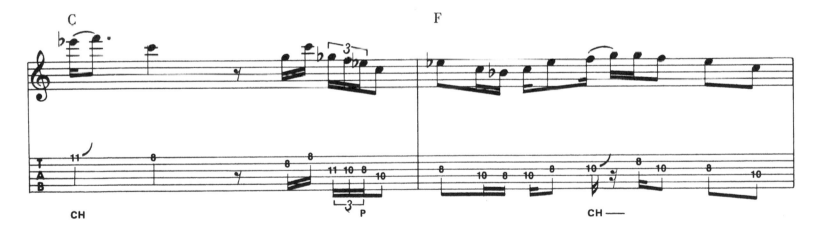

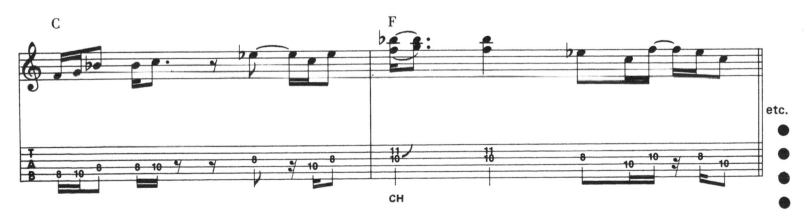

etc.

Incidentally, thousands of rock and R&B tunes end with a long vamp, which is a short progression repeated over and over; often it's this simple 1—4 progression you've just played.

Now take the rock progression in A (from Exercise No. 21) and play F# scales over the same rhythm part (F is a 6th above A) to get a more "major" sound. Exercise No. 24 illustrates this.

EXERCISE NO. 24 (LEAD)

ROCK PROGRESSION

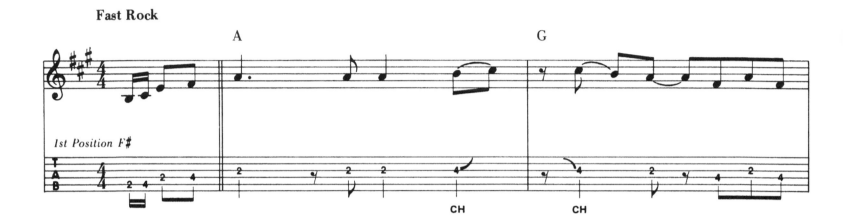

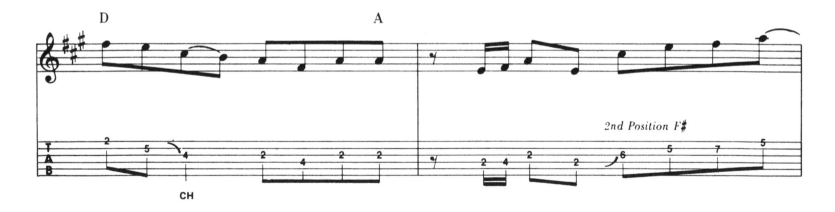

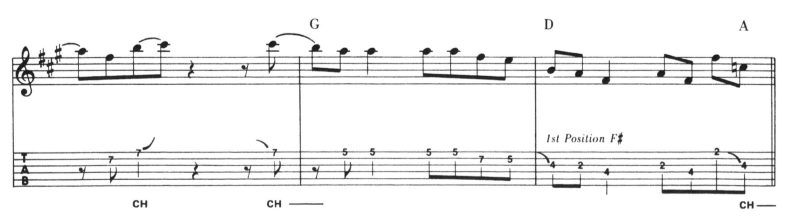

This major-sounding scale, a 6th above your actual key, works well for country-style improvisation. Exercise No. 25 is a common country-type progression in D, with the lead guitar playing B blues licks over it. The diagram below shows you one way to move up a 6th from D, automatically: you move up two frets from the D chord to a B minor, which sets you up to play the 1st position blues scale in B. This is what the guitar does in the first 8 bars of Exercise No. 25.

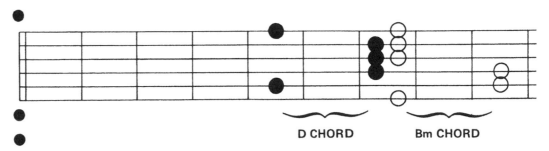

D CHORD   Bm CHORD

In the last 8 bars of Exercise No. 25 you move down 3 frets form the D chord, to a lower B minor, which sets you up to play the 4th position blues scale in B.

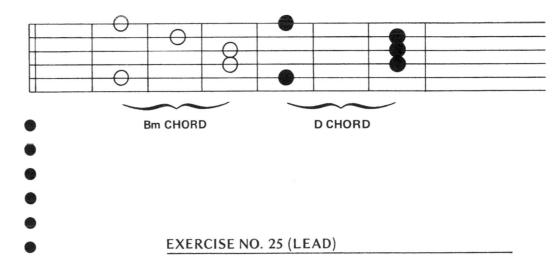

Bm CHORD   D CHORD

EXERCISE NO. 25 (LEAD)

Moderate Country Swing

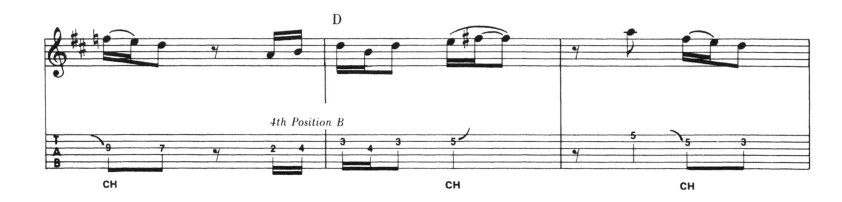

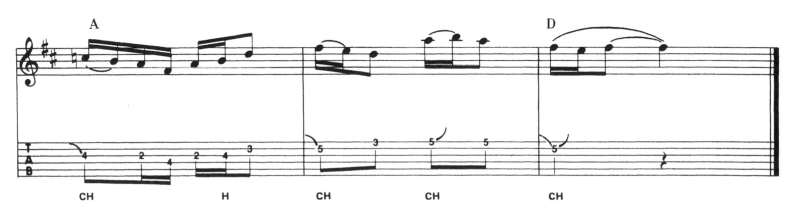

Now we can make some generalizations about moving up a 6th to get a more "major" sound. IT'S THE SAME AS MOVING FROM A MAJOR CHORD TO ITS RELATIVE MINOR, and here are some mechanical rules to follow:

—IF THIS IS YOUR STARTING CHORD (THE KEY YOU'RE IN): —

MOVE DOWN 3 FRETS AND PLAY THIS CHORD:
then play 1st position blues licks from this formation.

EXAMPLE: In the key of D, starting from this D chord.

move down 3 frets to this Bm:
and play 1st position scales.

— IF THIS IS YOUR STARTING CHORD (THE KEY YOU'RE IN):

MOVE UP 2 FRETS AND PLAY THIS CHORD:
Then, play 1st position blues licks from this formation.

OR MOVE DOWN 3 FRETS AND PLAY THIS CHORD:
And play 4th position licks from there.

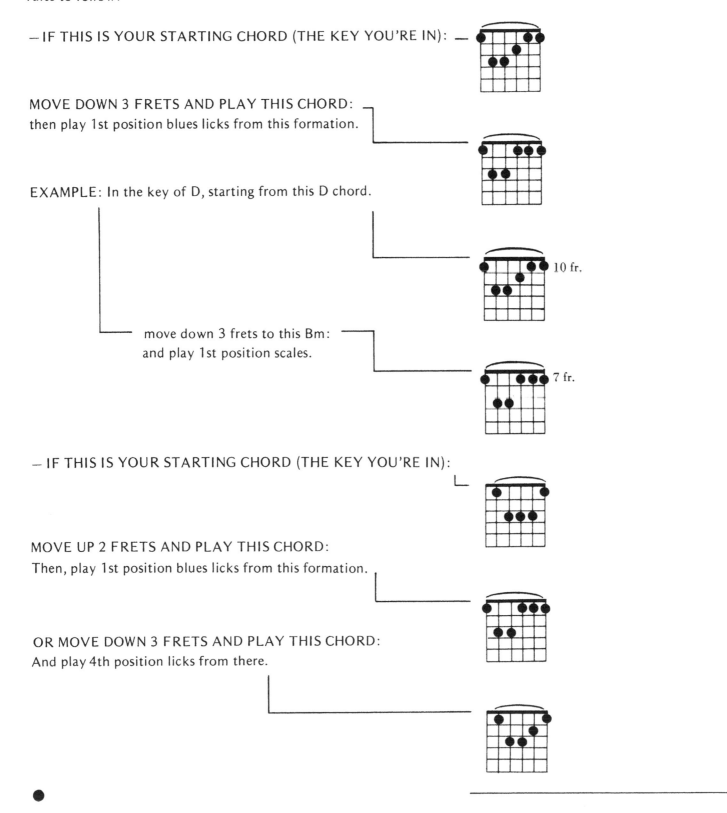

EXAMPLE: In the key of D, starting from this chord:

Move up 2 frets to this Bm:
And play 1st position scales

Or move down 3 frets to this Bm:
And play 4th position scales.

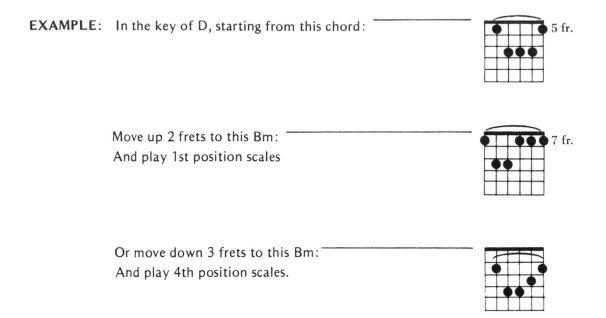

After some experimenting on your own, playing along with many different kinds of tunes, your ear will tell you whether to play blues scales in the actual key, or a 6th higher. Practice with records of rock, R&B, country music, soul music. You can play lead guitar to nearly anything using these techniques.

Before leaving the subject of rock, let's look at an example of heavy rock, or acid rock — the kind of guitar playing associated with Jimi Hendrix, Eric Clapton, Jimmy Page and others.

Acid-rock lead guitar is really blues guitar played with a lot of dynamics and intensity. The high volume and amp distortion, or fuzz tone effects, used in this music lend themselves to long, sustained, stretched-out notes. In Exercise No. 26 the lead guitar gets its intensity from just these techniques. The progression is in D, and the lead guitar plays D blues licks throughout. You'll need this new chord for the rhythm part:

EXERCISE NO. 26 (LEAD)

Slow, Heavy Rock

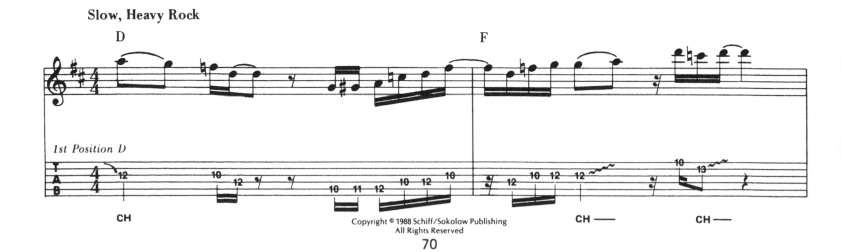

R&B: Listen to guitarists backing up current soul singers; their names are often listed in liner notes, and a few trendsetters to look for are Cornell Dupree, Eric Gale, Steve Cropper, Larry Carlton , Phil Upchurch, David T. Walker, Robben Ford—they're on many artists' records.

ROCK: Most of the big names in rock guitar play from a blues foundation, including Eric Clapton, Jimi Hendrix, Jimmy Page, Peter Frampton, Keith Richard (of the Rolling Stones), Jeff Beck, George Harrison. Much of what they do, as explained in this chapter, is blues guitar applied to non-blues progressions.

COUNTRY—ROCK: Guitarists playing with the Eagles, Linda Ronstadt, Crosby/Stills/Nash/Young (together or separately) or any soft rock or folk-rock groups, play a lot of blues licks in a folk or country context. They often use the "major" blues sounds described in this chapter. So do the hard-core country pickers like Roy Clark, or any guitarists backing up Merle Haggard, Buck Owens, Charlie Pride, or any of the country-western stars.

You can use the blues scales you've learned to play with a much more uptown sound. A lot of jazz, be-bop, soul and pop music is simply blues in disguise. Here are some new chords you should learn thoroughly to help understand the more sophisticated blues sounds:

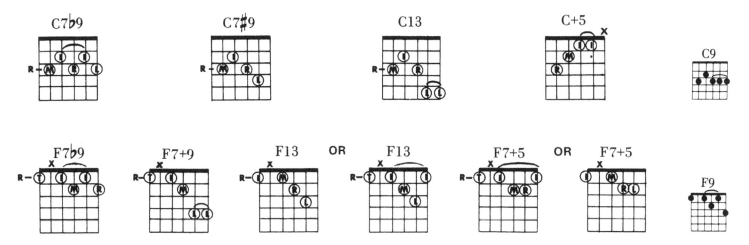

Notice that the first 4 chords are variations of the C9 chord which you already know, and the next 4 are variations of the F9 chord you've already used. Here are a few more:

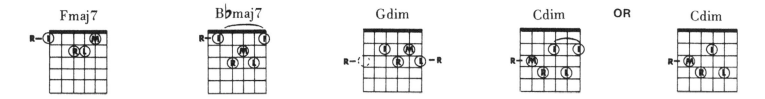

Exercise No. 27 is a popular blues progression in G that uses many of these new chords. The lead guitar plays G scales.

EXERCISE NO. 27 (RHYTHM)

Slow Blues

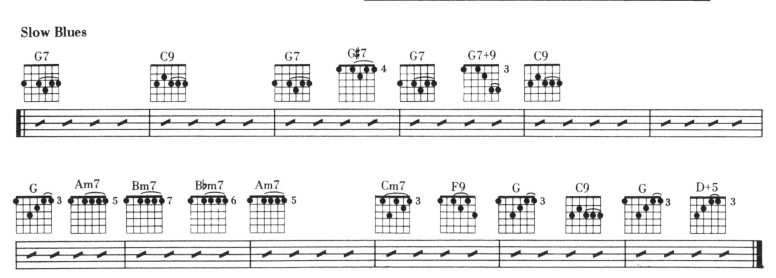

EXERCISE NO. 27 (LEAD)

Slow Blues

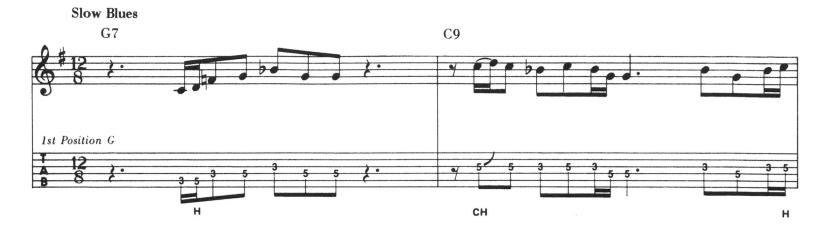

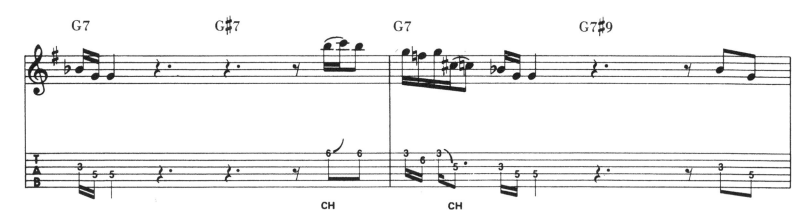

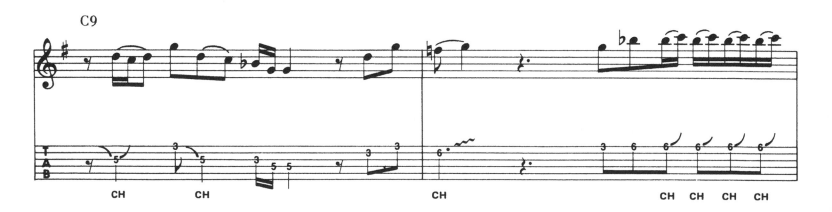

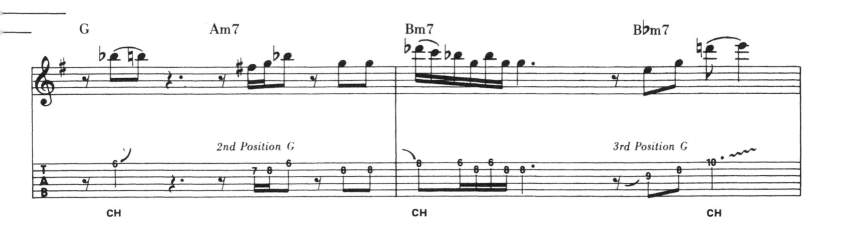

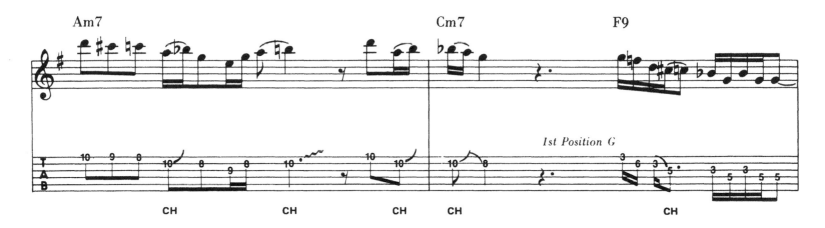

Here's how the blues you played in Exercise No. 19 can sound with some subtle chords.

EXERCISE NO. 28 (LEAD)

LEAD

Slow Blues

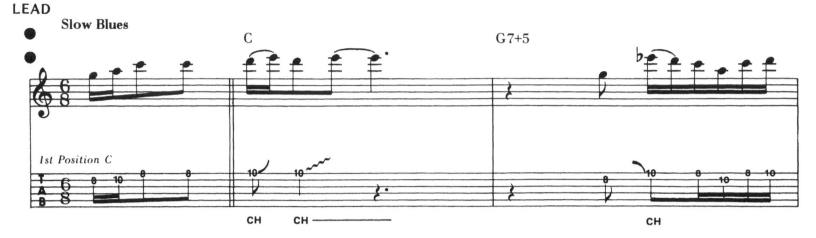

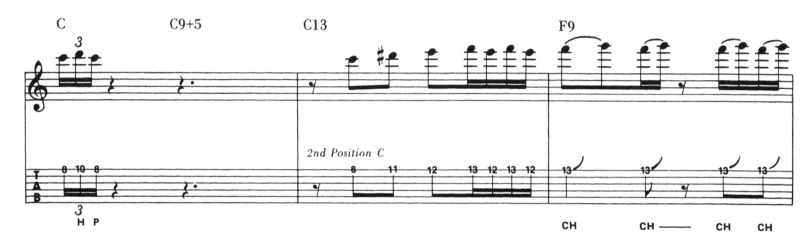

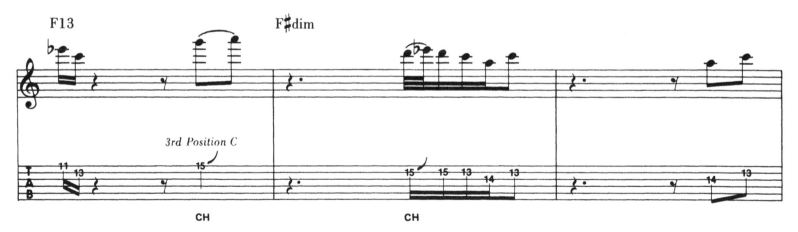

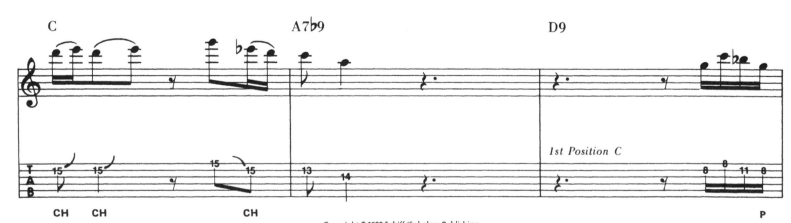

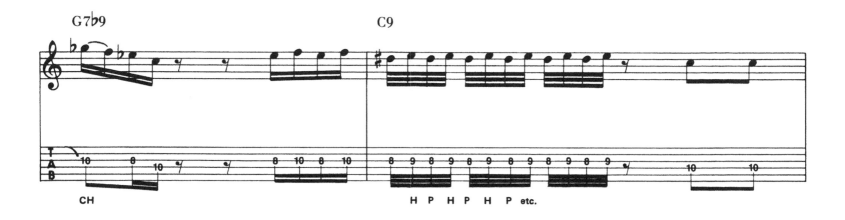

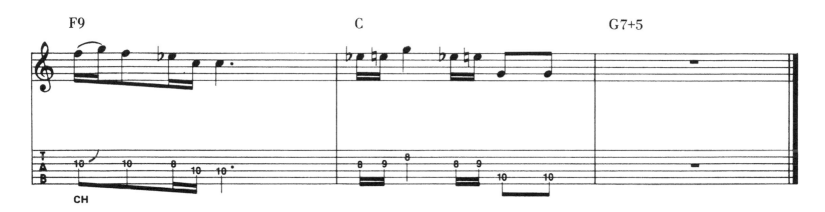

EXERCISE NO. 28 (RHYTHM)

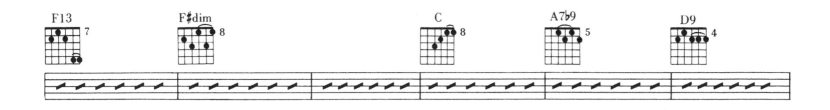

Slow Blues

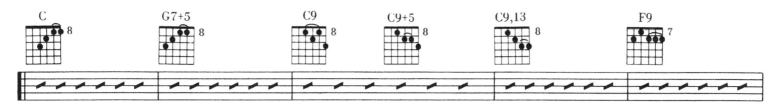

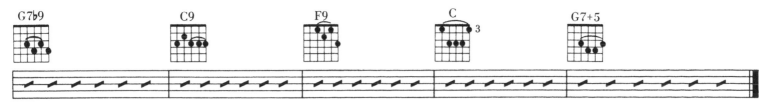

Here's an up-tempo blues, a 12-bar progression with a swing, or be-bop feeling. Despite the complicated changes, the lead guitar can play the usual blues. A lot of the chord movement here relates to the "circle of 5ths" progression described in the music theory appendix.

EXERCISE NO. 29 (RHYTHM)

Medium Swing Tempo

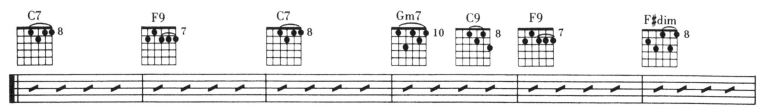

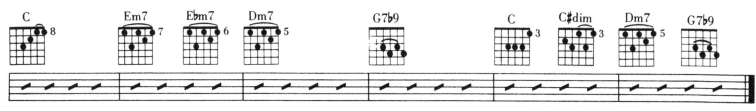

EXERCISE NO. 29 (LEAD)

Medium Swing Tempo

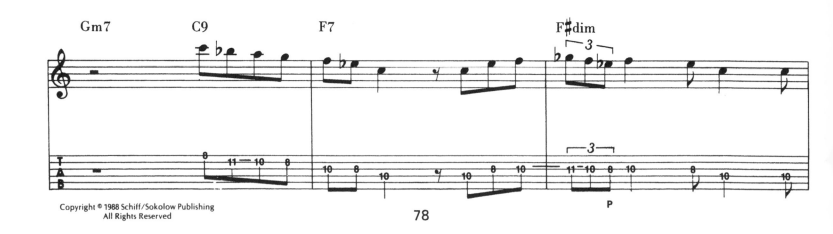

78

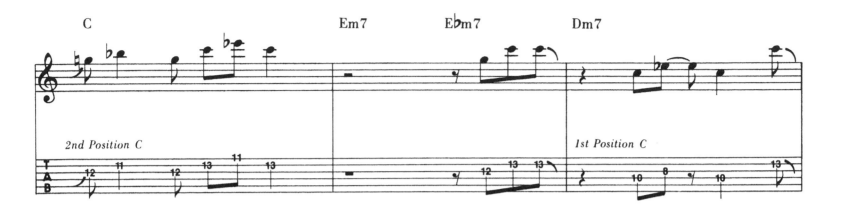

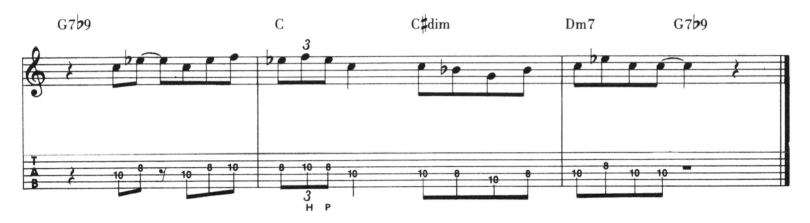

Here are a whole series of variations on that progression. They are all 12-bar blues.

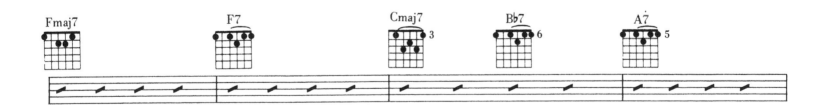

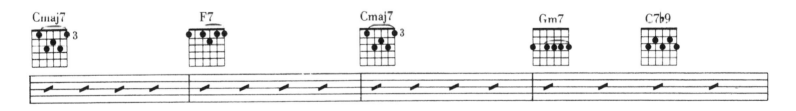

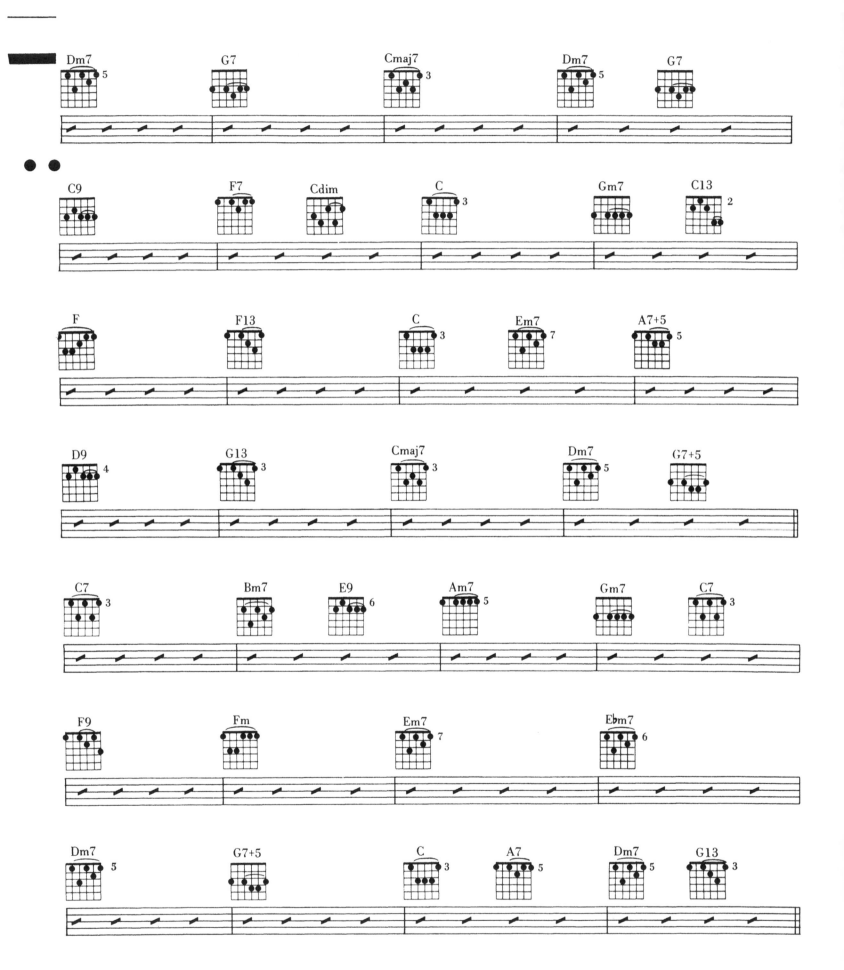

Many soul and blues singers are jazz oriented and the guitarists on their records deserve hearing. A few examples: Early Ray Charles, Esther Philips, Jimmy Witherspoon and instrumental albums by Grover Washington, Quincy Jones, The Jazz Crusaders.

Some amazing Western-swing guitarists can be heard playing jazzy blues licks on records of Bob Wills, Spade Cooley and, more recently, Asleep At The Wheel.

There's more to being a jazz guitarist than playing blues scales, but you'll be amazed how often the blues sounds appropriate to jazz progressions. There are several jazz progressions below, in the key of G. They are all variations on the jazz "turn-around," the chord progression that comes at the end of a musical phrase; but many complete tunes are based on these same changes. The G blues scales work very well over all these progressions. Exercise No. 30 gives you the rhythm parts and some sample lead parts; you try out your own G blues scales over them.

EXERCISE NO. 30 (RHYTHM)

A

EXERCISE NO. 30 (LEAD)

A

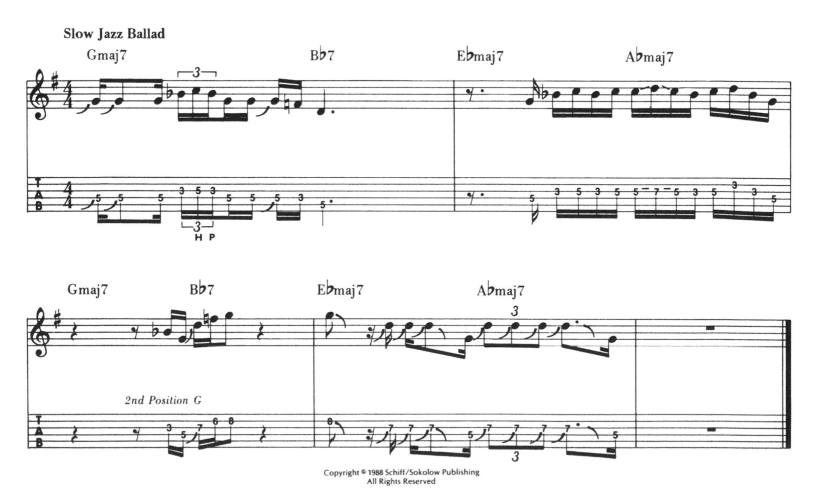

EXERCISE NO. 30 (RHYTHM)

B

Slow Jazz Ballad

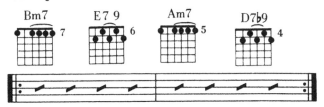

EXERCISE NO. 30 (LEAD)

B

Slow Jazz Ballad

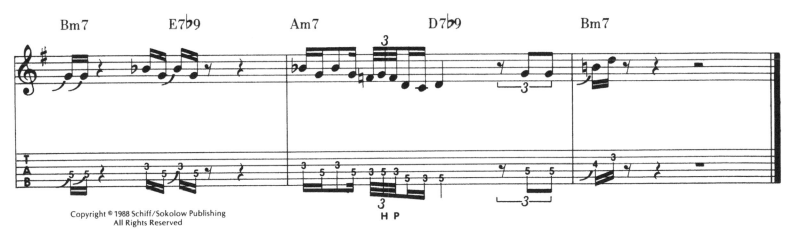

EXERCISE NO. 30 (RHYTHM)

C

Slow Jazz Ballad

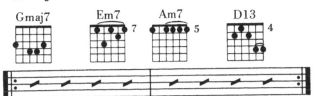

EXERCISE NO. 30 (LEAD)
C

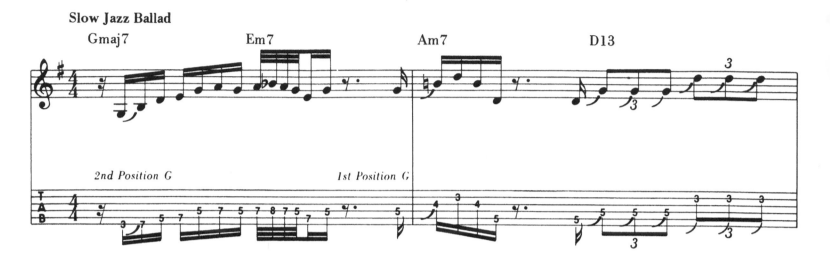

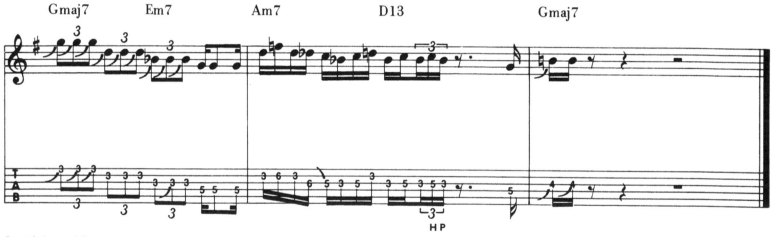

EXERCISE NO. 30 (RHYTHM)
D

Slow Jazz Ballad

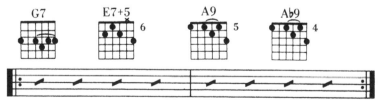

EXERCISE NO. 30 (LEAD) ● ● ● ● ● ● ● ● ● ● ● ● ● ● ● ● ● ●
D

● ● ●Slow Jazz Ballad

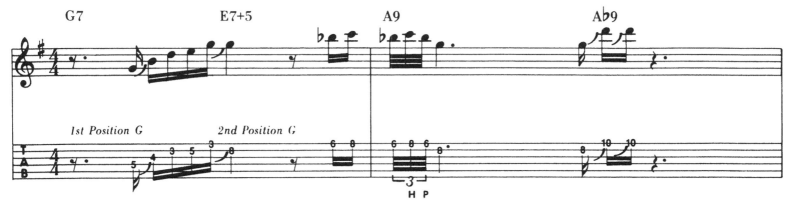

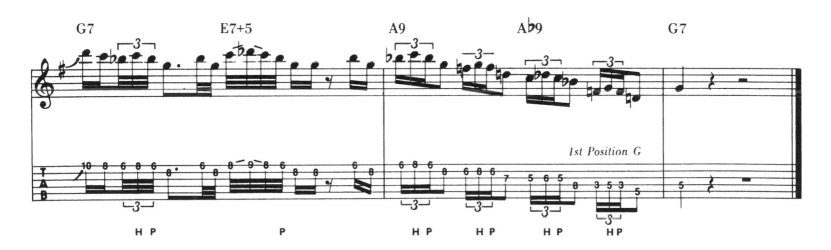

EXERCISE NO. 30 (RHYTHM)

E

Slow Jazz Ballad

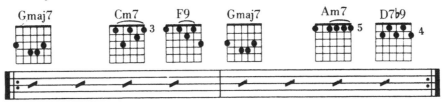

EXERCISE NO. 30 (LEAD)

E

● ● ● ● ● ● ● ● ● ● ● ● ● ●

Slow Jazz Ballad

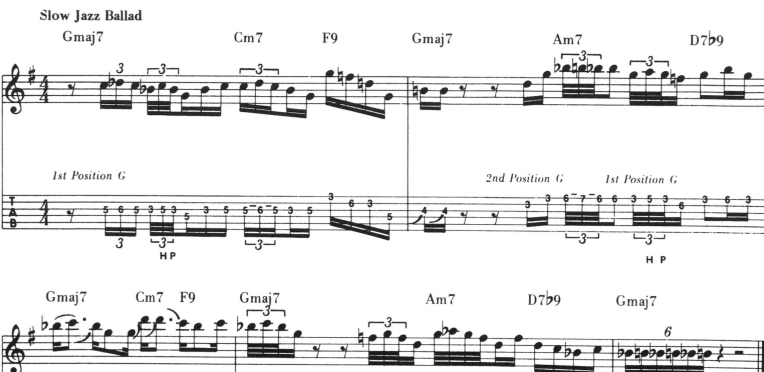

EXERCISE NO. 30 (RHYTHM)

F

Slow Jazz Ballad

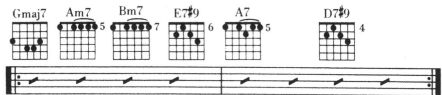

EXERCISE NO. 30 (LEAD)

F

Slow Jazz Ballad

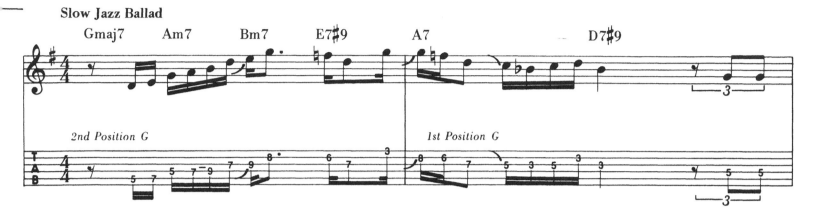

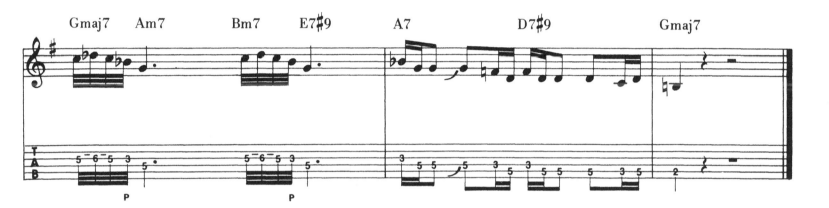

JAZZ WITH A BLUES FEELING
DISCOGRAPHY

Charlie Christian is a prime source and inspiration for all modern jazz guitarists, and his playing definitely evolves from the blues. So did the more recent styles of jazz giants like Wes Montgomery, Kenny Burrell, George Benson and Grant Green. George Benson's earliest records, before he played jazz, feature some amazing R&B guitar. He's probably the hottest new jazz guitarist around who has strong rhythm and blues roots. The late Wes Montgomery, one of Benson's main inspirations, was probably the most important player after Charlie Christian. See my book "Wes Montgomery Jazz Guitar Solos," distributed by Hal Leonard Publishing Corp. for Third Earth Publishing, Inc.

From the earliest recordings up to the present day, some of the most exciting and influential blues guitar music has involved the use of a slide or bottleneck. Many different types of slides and techniques for using them have evolved over the years . . . there are many varied tunings and just as many variations in the styles of music played with slides.

The earliest slides were broken-off bottlenecks, jackknives, shot glasses, lipstick tubes, anything that could fit over part of one of your fingers, or anything with an even, hard surface that could span the distance of several strings. A jackknife, or any object you have to hold in your left hand, prevents you from fretting chords or individual notes, so the bottleneck type of slide, which fits over your finger, is more versatile.

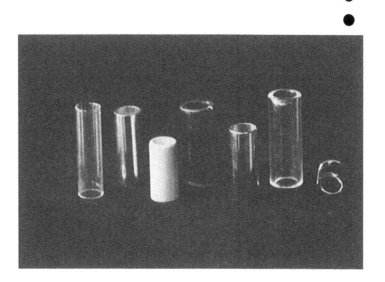

Today, most guitar stores offer an array of manufactured slides in different shapes and sizes, to fit over your ring finger or little finger.

Heavier glass tends to make less noise on the strings than metal—and it's more like a "real" bottleneck! But the slide to choose is the one you feel comfortable with when you start to play.

'OPEN A' TUNING

6 — E
5 — A
4 — E
3 — A
2 — C#
1 — E

The chart at the left tells you how to tune the strings up to an 'open A' tuning so that you're playing an A chord when you strum across open, unfretted strings. Starting from the regular tuning, look at your basic A chord:

A

Tune each of the fretted strings (the 2nd, 3rd and 4th strings) up two frets and you're in the 'open A' tuning.

The fingerboard chart below shows you an A scale that includes many open strings. The chart also indicates several barred chords: a D on the 5th fret, E on the 7th, and a high A on the 12th. When you use the slide to fret notes or to bar, place it directly over the desired fret-wire itself, not between the frets. Press lightly on the strings with the slide — do not bear down.

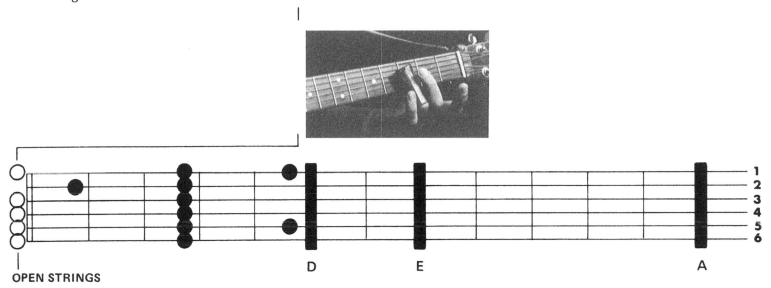

OPEN STRINGS   D   E   A

(Remember, the subdominant is 5 frets above the tonic, the dominant is 7 above.

—————————————————————— That's why the D and E bars work!) ——————————————

The barred chords, A, E and D can be made into sevenths by fretting the 1st and 2nd strings three frets above the bar:

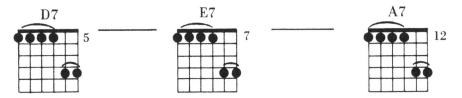

Exercise No. 31 is a finger-picking country blues in open A tuning. The thumb thumps out bass notes on the 5th string while the fingers pick out treble strings. The slide is used to fret most of the notes, but the fingers are occasionally used on bar chords or individual notes.

NOTE: slides performed with the bottleneck look like this in tablature:

pick 1st string on 3rd fret and slide down 1 or 2 frets

pick 2nd string on 3rd or 4th fret and slide up to 5th fret

pick 1st string on 3rd fret and slide up to 5th fret

EXERCISE NO. 31

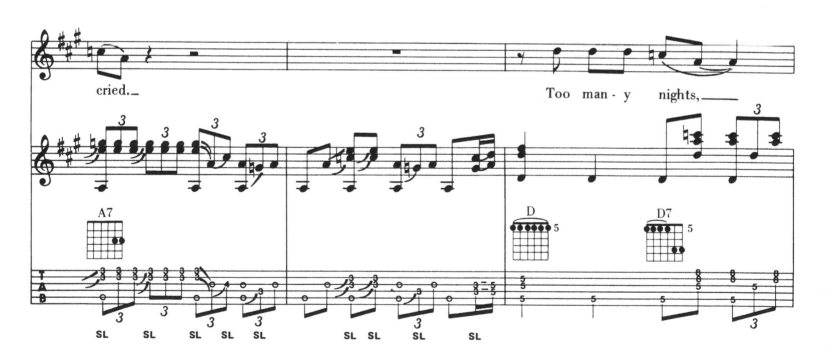

that I have lain_ a - wake and cried._ Ev-er

since you left me wom-an, you know I just can't___ be sat - is -

fied._

6 — D
5 — G
4 — D
3 — G
2 — B
1 — D

The "open G" tuning described to the left is just like the open A tuning, only two frets lower. So everything you learn in open A works the same in open G — only the names of the chords change. The bar on the 5th fret is a C chord, a bar on the 7th fret is D, the bar on the 12th fret is a G, and open strings give you a G chord. The seventh chords and the open scale you learned for Exercise No. 31 are the same, in the key of G.

To get to open G from the regular tuning, tune the 6th, 5th and 1st strings down 2 frets lower than usual.

The fingerboard chart below shows a G scale around the 12th fret that you'll use in Exercise No. 32. Remember, in A tuning you can use this exact scale for the key of A.

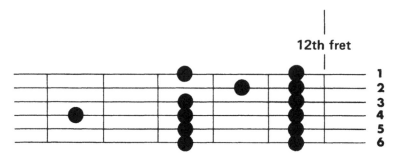

Not only can you use the open A scale in this tuning and call it a G scale, you can also move this scale up to the 12th fret and play it like this:

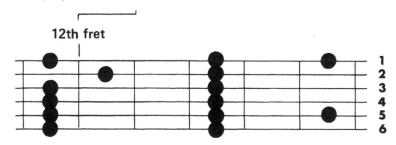

Naturally, in open A tuning this high scale becomes an A blues scale.

Exercise No. 32 is a G blues in which the lead guitar plays all the notes with a slide. Most of the lead is around the 12th fret, using the scales just described. It could be done just the same in A tuning in the key of A.

EXERCISE NO. 32　● ● ● ● ● ● ● ● ● ● ● ● ● ● ● ●

Slow Shuffle

Open G tuning

6 — D
5 — A
4 — D
3 — F♯
2 — A
1 — D

To get to open D from the regular tuning, tune the 6th and 1st and 2nd strings down 2 frets and tune the 3rd string down one fret.

You'll still have a 4 chord (G) by barring on the 5th fret, a 5 chord (A) by barring on the 7th fret, and a high tonic (D) on the 12th fret, but the scales you'll need are different from the G/A tuning. Here is an open D scale using many open strings:

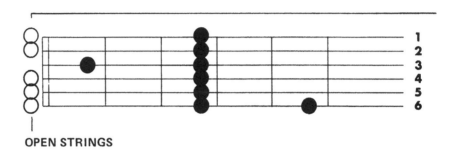

OPEN STRINGS

Exercise No. 33 is a fingerpicking country blues in open D, using fretted notes and slide. Notice how the guitar line often follows the vocal line. This is a popular technique in slide guitar. In fact, one of the main reasons for using a slide is to help the guitarist imitate the slurs and vibrato of a singing voice.

EXERCISE NO. 33

And I'm leav-in' in the morn-ing, I won't be back ___ 'til Fall. ___

And if I find an-oth-er wom-an, ___

I won't be back ___ at all.

Now we'll take the rock progression from Exercise No. 21 and play a lead guitar break over it in D tuning. Here's a blues scale you'll use—it's centered around the 12th fret.

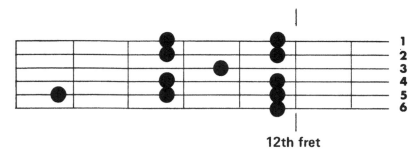

12th fret

Remember that you can also take the open scale used in Exercise No. 33 and move it up 12 frets, just as you moved the open G/A scale up 12 frets. This gives you two blues scales to work with, both centered around the 12th fret, as well as an open scale.

Play your two scales around the 12th fret, then try Exercise No. 34. The lead guitar is all slide in open D around the 12th fret. Notice the occasional use of octaves played on the 1st and 4th or 2nd and 5th strings.

EXERCISE NO. 34 (LEAD)

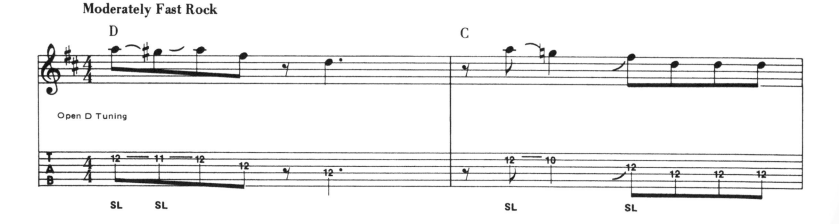

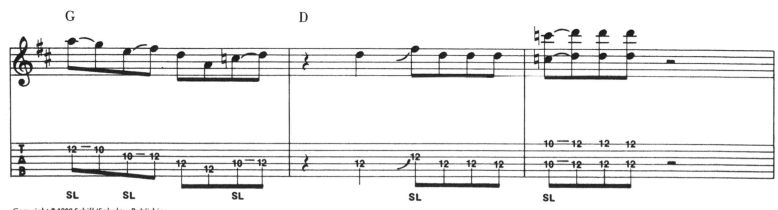

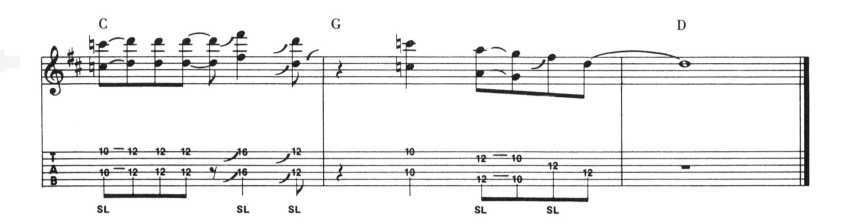

OPEN E TUNING

6 – E
5 – B
4 – E
3 – G#
2 – B
1 – E

The open E tuning is just like the open D, tuned up two frets. To get there from regular tuning, play the basic E chord: up 2 frets, and tune the 3rd string up one fret. Now tune the 5th and 4th strings one fret.

Just as with the G/A tuning, the scales and barred chords for open E and open D are the same — only the names change.

Exercise No. 35 is a blues in E tuning. The lead guitar is mostly centered around the 12th fret, so use the same scales you used in the last exercise.

EXERCISE NO. 35 (LEAD)

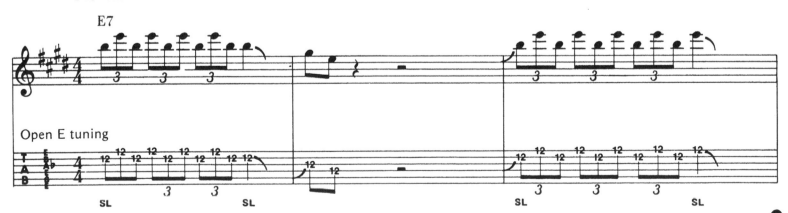

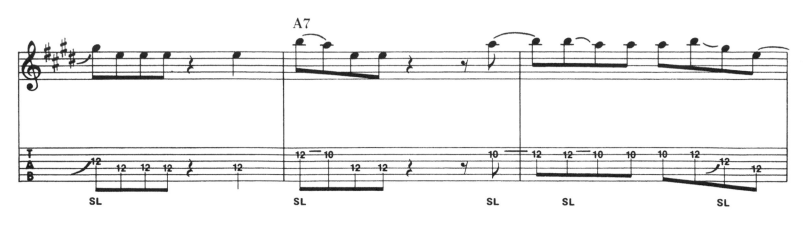

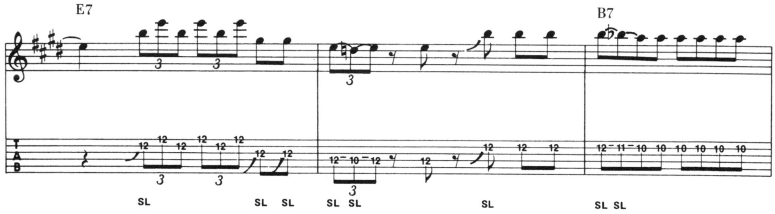

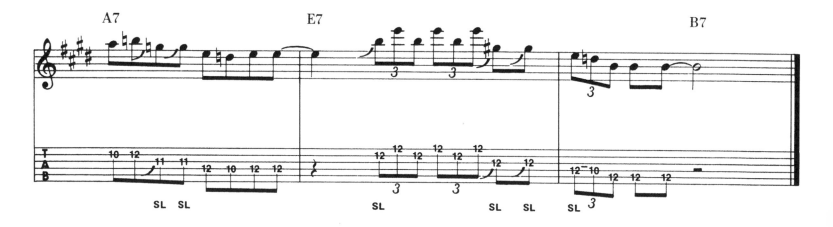

SLIDE IN THE REGULAR TUNING

Slide guitar in regular tuning is tricky—there are no open or barred chords to fall back on. If you're playing alone, you must keep coming back to solid chords. If you have some accompaniment you can use the basic blues positions you learned in the chapter on MODERN BLUES STYLES, and use the slide occasionally for stretched or choked strings.

Exercise No. 36 is a typical blues played in a fingerpicking country style, in regular tuning. It uses the E blues scale you learned way back in the chapter on COUNTRY BLUES, extended a bit. There's some playing up around the 12th fret, which is the 1st position (from the 5 basic blues positions). Lastly, there's a major triad (a 3-note chord) you can use on the 9th fret, which is part of this E chord: E 7 All the chords and many of the single notes are fretted, but the slide sound stands out.

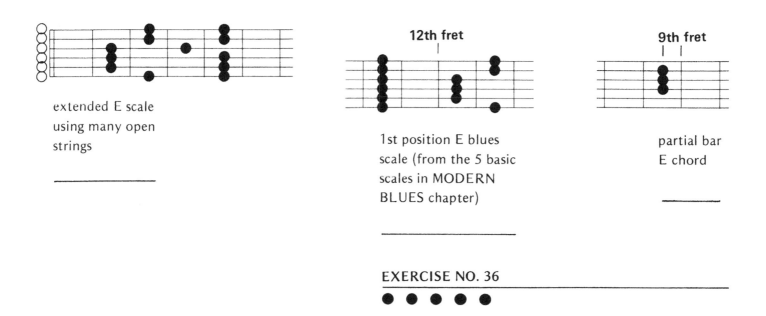

extended E scale
using many open
strings

12th fret

1st position E blues
scale (from the 5 basic
scales in MODERN
BLUES chapter)

9th fret

partial bar
E chord

EXERCISE NO. 36

● ● ● ● ●

Moderate Blues Shuffle

So long,___ I'm gon - na miss you some_

E7

A7

day.___ So long,___

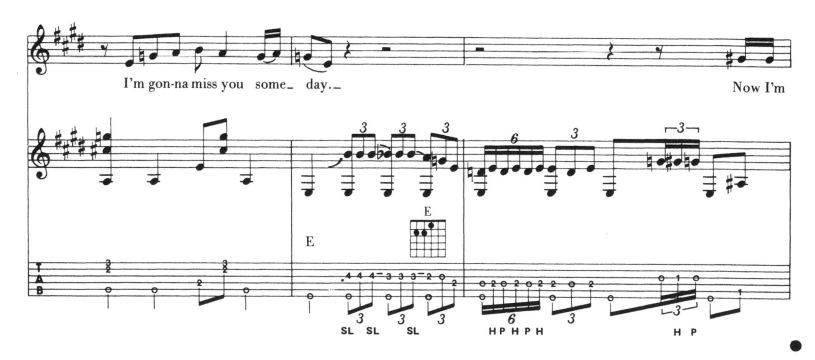

I'm gon-na miss you some_ day._ Now I'm

Many modern rock guitarists (George Harrison, Eric Clapton, Dicky Betts) use a slide in regular tuning to play very non-bluesy rock tunes. You can use the principle of "moving up a 6th" (described in the chapter on R&B, ROCK and COUNTRY ROCK) to do this. In Exercise No. 37 the progression is in the key of C and the lead guitar plays out of 'A' blues positions, often using the slide to stretch or slur notes. Remember, the basic blues positions are being used here. The slide is playing the same notes you would ordinarily fret, and many notes are not played with slide.

In the first part of the exercise the lead guitar plays the 2nd position A blues scale using the slide to stretch the top notes. For the second time around, move up to the 4th and 5th position A blues scales, way up the neck.

EXERCISE NO. 37 (LEAD)

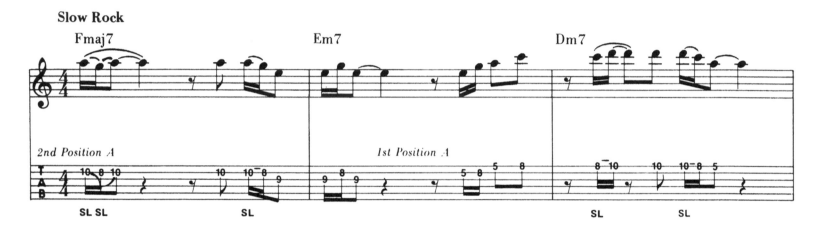

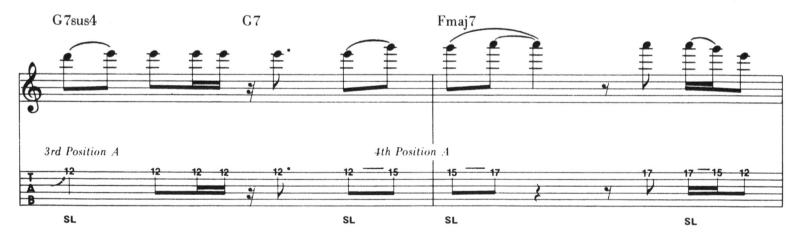

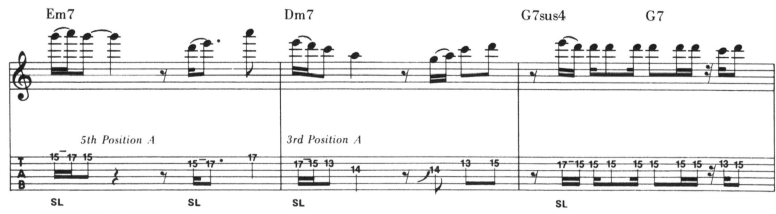

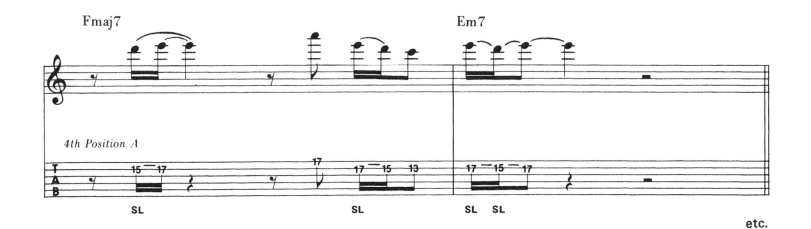

SLIDE GUITAR — DISCOGRAPHY

ACOUSTIC SLIDE GUITARISTS in the blues tradition: Robert Johnson (probably the most imitated slide player), Bukka White, Blind Lemon Jefferson, Son House, Mississippi Fred McDowell. More recent players are Ry Cooder, Taj Mahal, Stefan Grossman, all in the tradition, and Leo Kottke, who has his own bag!

ELECTRIC SLIDE GUITARISTS: Muddy Waters, Elmore James, early Albert Collins records, John Mayall and the Bluesbreakers (with Clapton), Johnny Winter.

ROCK MUSIC WITH SLIDE GUITAR: George Harrison (on his own records and on the last few Beatles albums), the Allman Brothers (Duane Allman and Dicky Betts), recent Eric Clapton, and Rolling Stones records on which Ry Cooder or Mick Taylor play.

SOME MUSIC THEORY

There are a few facts about chord relationships of which every blues player must be aware. First, there is the concept of a "key." A tune is played in a given key, and the tune will usually begin and end on the note and chord of its key. A song in the key of G will begin and end on a G chord. In the key of G, the G chord is called the tonic.

Five frets above the tonic is the sub-dominant, or "4 chord." (Count up from your key. Example: in the key of G, G=1, A=2, B=3, C=4, and so on.)

Seven frets above the tonic is the dominant, or "5 chord." (In the key of G, D is the 5 chord.)

The tonic, dominant and sub-dominant (one, five and four chords) are the three chords used in the 12-bar blues. So, once you know the key of a tune, you can "count up" to find which other chords you'll be using. The circle of fifths, pictured here, will help you do this. When you move clockwise one step, you are going from a tonic to a dominant (moving up a fifth) — from G to D, for example. When you move counter-clockwise you are going from a tonic to a sub-dominant (up a fourth) — from G to C.

If a tune is in the key of E, the circle of fifths tells you that A (the four chord) and B (the five chord) will be the other two chords in the tune.

RELATIVE MINORS: The minor chord inside the circle is the relative minor to its companion note outside (Em is the relative minor to G). It is a sixth above the tonic — two frets above the dominant. (If G is the "one chord" then count up: G[1], A[2], B[3], C[4], D[5], E[6] to arrive at the chord that is a sixth higher.)

If a tune uses a minor chord, it will probably be the relative minor . . . or the relative minor to the dominant or sub-dominant. That's why there are so many Em, Am and Dm chords in all the C swing tunes (in the chapter BLUES WITH A JAZZ FEELING). Am is relative to C, Dm to F (the sub-dominant) and Em to G (the dominant).

You'll use your knowledge of relative minors in the section on country-rock, R & B, and rock when you need to move "up a 6th" in order to play scales that have a more "major" sound. You simply move to the relative minor and play blues scales in that key. If the tune is in A, for example, go to F#m and play F# scales.

CIRCLE OF FIFTHS

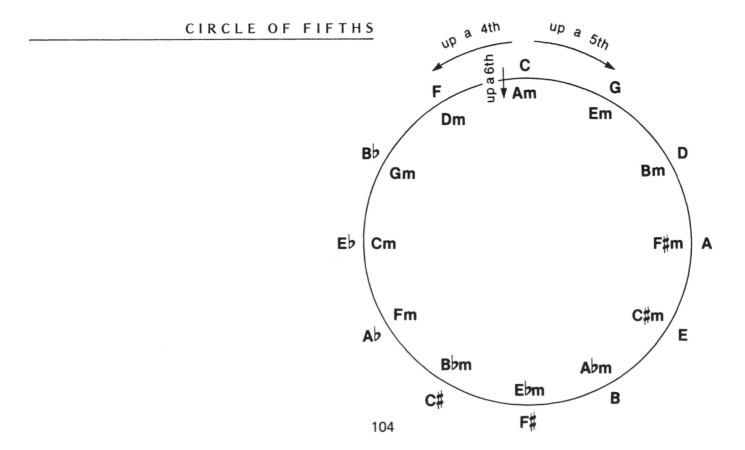

Many pop and jazz progressions which have more than the usual three chords move "in a circle of fifths." For example, a tune in the key of G might jump to an E and then go counter-clockwise along the circle to arrive back at G, giving you a progression like this: G/E/A/D/G. You'll find this type of chord movement in the progressions in the chapter of JAZZ WITH A BLUES FEELING, in which I point out that you can usually play regular blues lines against a circle-of-fifths type of tune.

After playing many tunes in different keys you'll start to feel, instinctively, where the four and five chords and the relative minor are found. The circle of fifths type of movement becomes very familiar too, in time. You will save yourself the most time, however, if you study the circle of fifths in the first place. Pick any key and play the four and five chords and relative minor to that key . . . switch keys and do the same, and try to hear the sounds of the different chord relationships.

BUYING A GUITAR

First, there's the question of which guitar to choose: a steel string, nylon string, 12-string, electric . . . to name a few of the alternatives! You'll find lots of choices within each category, too.

The blues can be played on any of these, so it's mainly a matter of personal preference: which sound do you like best? There are practical considerations, though, and traditions. Most of the rural country-blues pickers used a steel-string guitar, and you can best imitate their sound by playing the same guitar they played. Bottleneck players often use a steel string guitar with very high action or very heavy strings to avoid the fret noise a bottleneck can make, but the action (the distance between the strings and fretboard) can easily and inexpensively be altered to your taste on any guitar. Many country blues pickers, especially slide players, use a National Steel or Dobro guitar with an all metal body (you may have seen Taj Mahal playing one in the Sounder movies). But be careful not to get a "square neck" Dobro, which can only be used as a lap instrument—they're used in country-western and bluegrass music.

Most modern blues is played on the electric guitar. Jazz-oriented players and the older blues players (like B.B. King) prefer a hollow body electric, which has some acoustic sounds as well as electric. But the solid body guitars, especially the Gibson Les Paul and Fender Telecaster, are more popular with rock players. These lend themselves to high-volume playing and lots of sustained, stretched-out notes. If you want to play slide guitar on an electric, it's nice to have high tension on the strings, and high action.

If you seriously want to sound like someone in particular, it helps a lot to play the same kind of guitar they play. These days, with all the music magazines and knowledgable music stores around, it's not hard to find out who's playing what instrument on which record. But if you're looking for your own, personal sound, go to one of the big guitar stores that carries acoustic and electric guitars and play everything you see! Get the best instrument you can afford—and one that grabs you—because you'll practice more on it than you would on your second choice.

WHAT TO LOOK FOR IN A GUITAR

Make sure the guitar's neck is straight by looking straight down the neck (as if looking through a gun-sight) and by playing the notes high up the neck to see if they are in tune. Some bowed necks can be repaired, but the store selling you the instrument should take care of it . . . otherwise, forget it!

Good instruments improve with age and with a lot of use, so don't automatically rule out instruments with scratches or signs of wear. But don't let anyone but an expert re-finish or touch-up a scratched guitar because the tone can be very adversely affected. Also, serious cracks will affect the tone of the instrument.

If the action is high and the strings hard to fret as a result, only buy the guitar if the store or someone you trust will change the action for you.

Obviously, the most important thing is that the instrument feels good when you play it, and sounds the way you want it to.

BUYING A GUITAR

All these guitars can be used to play the blues - their "specialty" is listed as well.

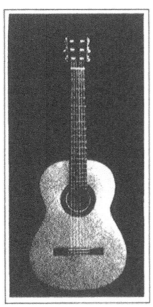

NYLON STRING ACOUSTIC
Folk - Classical - Flamenco

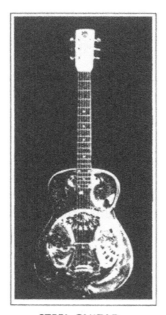

STEEL GUITAR
Country Blues - Folk - Slide

STEEL STRING ACOUSTIC
Folk - Country

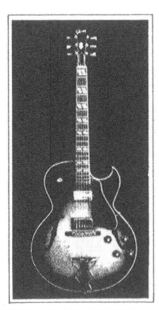

HOLLOW BODY ELECTRIC
Jazz

F-HOLE or "ARCH-TOP" ACOUSTIC
Swing

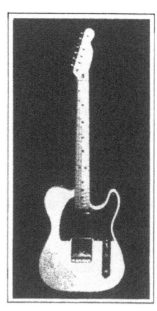

SOLID BODY ELECTRIC
Rock - Country

12 STRING ACOUSTIC
Folk - Country Blues

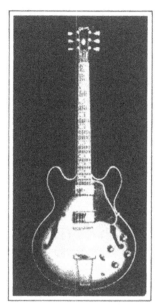

SEMI-HOLLOW BODY ELECTRIC
Rock - R&B

SOLID BODY ELECTRIC
Rock - Country

CHORD DICTIONARY

A

A7

A7

B7

C

C7

D

D7

E

E7

E7

F

F7

G

G7

107

The root of each of these chords is circled heavily so that once you learn the 5th and 6th string notes up and down the fingerboard (by studying the fingerboard diagram below) you can use each chord in many places. Example: the F chord below can be moved up 2 frets to become a G. Moved up to the 8th fret, it's a C (because the 6th string on the 8th fret is a C).

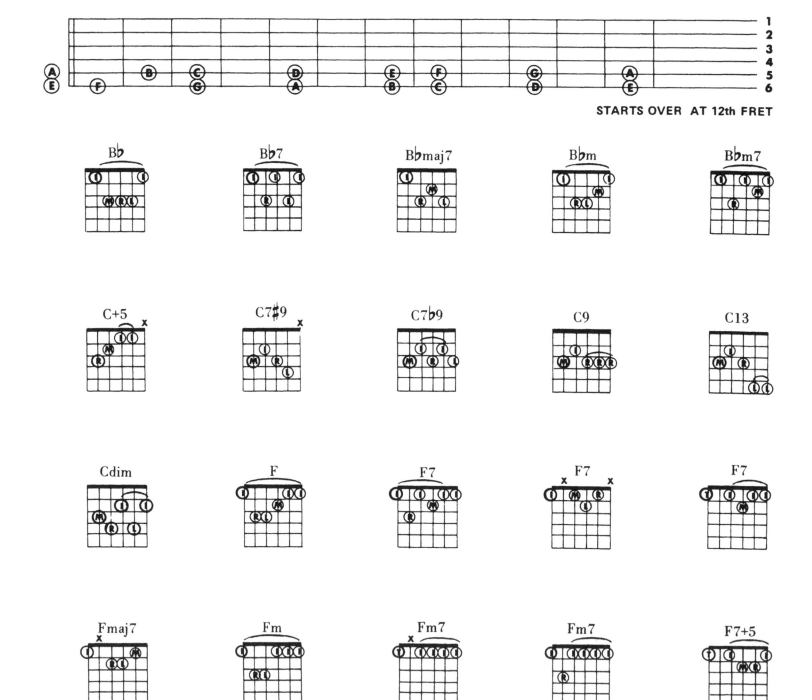

108

F7+5

F7♯9

F7♭9

F9

F9

F9

F13

F13

Gdim

All the notes are circled in the G° and C° chords (G diminished and C diminished). That's because a diminished chord has many uses—any note in the chord can be the root note. The G° can also be used as a C#°, E°, or B♭°.

Many thanks to the musicians who accompanied me on the tape: Jim Fielder (Bass) and Dennis Alexander (Drums).

Thanks also to Ginger O'Neil for her photography; and to the Bob Baxter Guitar Workshop for their photographs and for some of the fine instruments they let us use. Thanks, too, to Walecki's Music, who let us photograph their guitars.

— Fred Sokolow

Art Direction - Ron Mason
Design - Bill Reynolds